STRETCHING
HIDE

STRETCHING
HIDE

Dale Lakevold
Darrell Racine

Stretching Hide
first published 2007 by
Scirocco Drama
An imprint of J. Gordon Shillingford Publishing Inc.
© 2007 Dale Lakevold and Darrell Racine
Reprinted March 2010

Scirocco Drama Editor: Glenda MacFarlane
Cover artwork by Kristine Dmytrak/Relish Design Ltd.
Cover design by Terry Gallagher/Doowah Design Inc.
Photo of Dale Lakevold by Derek Gunnlaugson
Printed and bound in Canada

We acknowledge the financial support of the Manitoba Arts Council, The Canada
Council for the Arts and the Government of Canada through the Book Publishing
Industry Development Program (BPIDP) for our publishing program.

Library and Archives Canada Cataloguing in Publication

Lakevold, Dale, 1957-
    Stretching hide / Dale Lakevold, Darrell Racine.

A play.
ISBN 978-1-897289-26-6

    I. Racine, Darrell, 1961- II. Title.

PS8573.A38134S87 2007   C812'.6   C2007-905759-4

J. Gordon Shillingford Publishing
P.O. Box 86, RPO Corydon Avenue, Winnipeg, MB Canada R3M 3S3

Acknowledgments

David Copelin, ScriptLab, Robb Mowbray, Theatre BC, Janet Michael, David Ross, Yvette Nolan, Native Earth Performing Arts, Department of English (Brandon University), Di Brandt, Rosanne Gasse, Reinhold Kramer, Lisa Robson, Barbara Rose, Lorraine Mayer, Gender & Women's Studies (Brandon University), Scott Grills, Faculty of Arts (Brandon University), Jan Mahoney, Calle Lakevold, Vanya Hanson, Cindy Hanson, Bill and Clara Lakevold, Tom Racine, Doug Racine, Mildred Racine, Carol, Leah Laplante, Ivy Corbel, Marsha Knight, Glenda MacFarlane, Gord Shillingford, and Mike Bell. Special thanks to Rory Runnells, Manitoba Association of Playwrights, Bruce McManus, Ulla Ryum, Harry Rintoul, Per Brask, and Chris Johnson. Thank you to the Manitoba Arts Council for financial support in the development of the script. Thank you to all the actors, dramaturges, directors, and other theatre artists who participated in the various workshops and readings of the script, and especially to Theatre Projects Manitoba, Ardith Boxall, Rea Kavanagh, Arne McPherson, Grant Guy, and the wonderfully talented and creative cast and crew of the Winnipeg premiere.

About the Authors

Darrell Racine's play *Misty Lake*, co-written with Dale Lakevold, has been produced in Brandon, Winnipeg, Calgary, and Prince George, and has toured Northern Manitoba. In Calgary it was produced at the 2002 Crazy Horse Aboriginal Theatre Festival with Tina Keeper and Tantoo Cardinal in the cast. *Misty Lake* was published in a new edition in 2006 by Loon Books. He is a graduate of Harvard and Cambridge, and he is currently completing his doctorate at Oxford. He is a Métis from the Turtle Mountains in Southwestern Manitoba and lives in Brandon. He teaches in the Department of Native Studies at Brandon University.

Dale Lakevold's plays include *Wild Geese* and *Cross Creek* (University of Winnipeg), *L-Love's Body* and *Never Never Mind, Kurt Kurt Cobain* (Theatre Projects Manitoba), *Misty Lake* (Root Sky and Crazy Horse), and *Making L-Love's Body* (Brandon University). His audio theatre installation "Notes for a Speech on (Canadian) Flagmaking" was produced at the Art Gallery of Southwestern Manitoba in 2003 by the Brandon Arts Collective. He was nominated for the John Hirsch Award for Most Promising Writer in Manitoba in 1999. He is a member of the Manitoba Association of Playwrights and the Playwrights Guild of Canada. He lives in Brandon where he teaches at Brandon University.

Production Information

Stretching Hide was premiered by Theatre Projects Manitoba, in association with Root Sky Productions, in Winnipeg, on November 1, 2007 with the following cast and crew:

MARTEN: .... Eric Blais
FRANK: .... Ryan Cunningham
ALFRED: .... Thomas Hauff
MARIE: .... Paula-Jean Prudat
CLARA: .... Daria Puttaert
SANDY: .... Jan Skene
EUGENE: .... Jonathan Fisher

Director: Arne MacPherson
Production Design: Grant Guy
Lighting Design: Hugh Connacher
Stage Manager: Natalie Woodburn-Heron and Michelle Lagassé
Apprentice Stage Manager: Ivory Seol
Live fiddling provided by Jesse Hull

Stretching Hide was first read at a Manitoba Association of Playwrights' Open Door session in Winnipeg in December 2000. It was later read as part of the Off the Page Reading Series produced by Script Lab at Harbourfront in Toronto on April 13, 2002. It received a workshop and reading at the Weesagachak Begins to Dance Festival XVI from September 25-October 4, 2003, by the Native Earth Performing Arts Company in Toronto. It received an award for Best Full-Length Play by Theatre BC in its 16th Annual Canadian Playwriting Competition for 2004 and given a workshop and reading at the Theatre BC New Play Festival in Kamloops, BC, from April 1-3, 2005. It also had a reading on August 15, 2005, at the Gender and Canadian Values in the 21st Century Conference at Brandon University.

Characters

All characters are Métis with the exception of Sandy and Clara.

Place, Time, and Setting

The Willows, a small Métis community near Saskatoon, Saskatchewan. June 29–July 3 (Thursday–Monday). Late 1990s.

FRANK's kitchen is in his grandpa's old house, a typical Métis house from the 1950s.

ALFRED's fur shack is the size of a small garage. It hasn't been painted or repaired in thirty years. The shack is crammed with whatever a trapper and hunter has accumulated over the years.

THE KID's shack is a small one-room house without plumbing or insulation. It is full of cast-off furniture and items of all variety.

Playwrights' Statement and Production Notes

Stretching Hide is the second play in a series that we are writing about Aboriginal culture and history in Canada. We began in the late 1990s with *Misty Lake*, a play that examines the residential school experience and the process of healing. In *Stretching Hide*, we're attempting to show other paths by which individuals and communities can come to terms with unresolved events in their past.

Set

A full set might be built along the following lines.

Frank's kitchen has an arborite table, chairs, plywood cupboards made locally, cast iron wood stove and woodbox, electric stove, tea kettle, box radio, and linoleum floor worn away in places. Catholic paraphernalia, including a cross made from burnt matches and a painting of the Last Supper, is found throughout. An electric frying pan is on the counter. Off the kitchen is a small living room that would contain a black and white TV, family photographs, couch and armchair, and throw rug. Bare bulb lighting. One door leads off the kitchen to a bedroom offstage. Another door leads outside. On the wall by the door is a gunrack with a .22 in it.

Alfred's fur shack has a large door, a window, a small wood stove, a few kitchen chairs, and an old kitchen table that serves as a fur table. On the walls would hang wildlife pictures, calendar women, licence plates, tools, animal traps, gunrack and guns, snowshoes, and a snowmobile suit. Other items might include a chainsaw, ice pick, shovels, axes, knives, radio, fridge, frying pan and pots, and tins of tobacco. Cases of beer are stacked against one wall. The shack is lit by a single light bulb inside a beaten-up metal shade that dangles over the fur table. A framed photo of Alfred's late wife hangs on a wall.

Marten's shack has a wood stove; a window with burlap curtain; and an open cupboard lined with canned meat, canned potatoes, evaporated milk, sugar, peanut butter, Kraft Dinner, lard, coffee, tea, and jars of canned fruit and pickled vegetables. The shack is lighted by a bulb hooked up to a car battery. It has a wooden picnic table, a chair, a wooden crate for sitting, a front seat (on cinder blocks.) from a pickup truck, a binder twine clothesline, a bundle of willow branches, a few stretching boards, and a set of deer antlers on a blue Coleman cooler (riddled with bullet holes.).

A worn hide-a-bed love seat is unfolded in the corner. Clothes are hung on spikes. The Kid has a chemical pail for water. A large wall-hanging (a large rug, perhaps) with the image of a deer hangs on one wall. He's salvaged a number of other items over the years: hubcaps, snowmobile engine parts, car tire, birdhouse, and stuffed mink.

Characters

Marten ("The Kid") is able to live on his own, despite an impairment that he's had from infancy. His mental disability has given the community an excuse to treat him arbitrarily. Sometimes he's been neglected; sometimes he's been put in danger; most often he's been treated like a child who doesn't know any better. He's never been fully respected. Even so, he wants to be liked. And he wants to please everyone.

Music

Two Métis musicians—a fiddler and a guitarist—perform original and traditional compositions throughout the play. Music should be incorporated fully into this story. The musicians should have their own place on stage.

Act One

Scene One

Lights dim to black. Thursday night. Moonlight falls on MARTEN who is watching a deer from a clump of willows. Suddenly ALFRED appears beside him. MARTEN crouches lower to avoid being seen. He watches ALFRED and the deer. ALFRED watches the deer, his head moving back and forth slightly as if looking through branches. When the deer has moved into position, ALFRED raises his .30-30 to his shoulder. He holds the deer in his sights for about five seconds. Blackout/gunshot.

Scene Two

Friday noon. Lights up on MARTEN's shack just as MARTEN fires a stone from his slingshot at a large wall-hanging of a deer.

MARTEN: I got you again.

He inspects the deer then speaks quietly, taking the deer into his confidence.

I could of got you last night, you know—down there at the Ring Field. I saw you there, just eating that alfalfa. That's right. I was watching you real close.

Low light on ALFRED in the fur shack. The action is simultaneous with MARTEN's scene. ALFRED's gun and antlers lie on the fur table. He pours a drink. He inspects the horns, hangs them up, and admires them.

MARTEN: But you know something? I wouldn't of cut those antlers off you like Alfred did. He just left you lying there in that alfalfa.

I wouldn't of done that.

No, I would of taken all your meat—

I would of fed everybody in the whole Willows with it.

MARIE enters. She has a brown paper bag.

He loads his slingshot. He aims at the deer.

If I had my own gun, that is—

MARIE: Marten.

Startled, MARTEN fires the stone wildly. She ducks.

Whoa there. I didn't know bringing a bag of chicken feed could be so dangerous.

MARTEN: You got some chicken feed?

MARIE: Yeah, Eugene got some for you.

MARTEN: Eugene's gonna sell me his gun.

MARIE: Is that right? And what would you do with that?

MARTEN: Well, I'd hunt. Cause I can't go hunting without no gun.

MARIE: You don't need any meat anyway. You got those chickens—if you got any left, that is.

MARTEN: What do you mean?

MARIE: I mean the way you keep on feeding that mink—

MARTEN: I'm gonna get that mink that's been killing all my chickens.

MARIE: Eugene says that mink's gotten so fat he looks like a beaver.

MARTEN: That mink's as good as dead. Cause I know where he's coming in and where he's going out.

MARIE: Yeah, and you can choke him to death when he gets himself stuck in that hole.

MARTEN: No, I'm gonna choke him with this. I'm gonna set this old trap of Alfred's—just like this—

            He picks up the leghold trap and goes through the motions of trapping his mink.

            I'm gonna set it right by that hole in the floorboards—right where he comes into the chicken coop. And he's gonna come flying through that hole, and he's gonna run right into that trap. And then… SNAP!—

            He slaps a willow on the table top. Lights down at the fur shack.

            And he'll just be flippin and floppin there in that trap—

            He's flipping and flopping his hands frantically.

            I betcha those chickens'll have themselves a party.

MARIE: Yeah, and you'll be able to have one too on the money you'll get from that hide. Isn't that right?

MARTEN: Forty-five bucks! (*He slaps the table.*) That's what that pelt's gonna fetch me.

            He goes through the motions of skinning.

            I'll skin him out. Oh yeah, I'll scrape that hide of his, and then I'll stretch him out—real good and tight.

MARIE: You gotta catch that mink before you can stretch him.

MARTEN: Oh, I'll catch him, and then I'll go see that fur buyer over there at Peter Allbright's store every Sunday. And then I'll take that 45 bucks over to Eugene. I'm gonna get my first gun—Eugene's old gun.

MARIE: So he promised you that.

MARTEN: Yeah, he was over here last night and told me I was ready.

> *MARIE picks up an empty beer bottle left over from EUGENE's visit.*

MARIE: And I suppose he said you were ready to start drinking, too.

MARTEN: No, Eugene said I couldn't drink until I got my first deer.

MARIE: He told you that?

MARTEN: Well, kinda. He said we'd have to celebrate.

MARIE: If he starts celebrating, you stay home. The last time he celebrated I had to go pick him up in Fort Qu'Appelle and his truck in Foam Lake.

MARTEN: I don't go nowhere. I just wanna go hunting.

MARIE: And you'll get your chance.

MARTEN: That's right. Franky promised he'd take me. And then I'll get my deer. *(He aims his empty slingshot at the calendar.)*

SANDY: *(SANDY enters.)* Jesus christ, what the hell you doin firing stones inside your own house?

MARTEN: I wasn't firing no stones. See?

> *He shows her the empty sling and looks at MARIE.*

MARIE: He was just…practicing.

SANDY: Go practice outside then. No one fires slingshots inside their house. Now, come on, use your brain.

MARTEN: But Mom—

SANDY: You put that slingshot away and come up for something to eat. I can't wait around all day.

MARTEN: I'm not hungry—

SANDY: Marie brought us over some meat Eugene got us.

MARTEN: I should be getting that meat for us—

SANDY: Don't you worry about that—

MARTEN: I'm gonna get that gun from Eugene. He promised me—

SANDY: You will not be getting any gun. You know what happened the first time.

MARTEN: That was an accident.

SANDY: Yes, I know it was an accident. But you don't know how to use a gun.

MARIE: You gotta quit blaming that kid for everything.

SANDY: I'm not blaming him. That's just the way he is.

MARIE: That's right, and he's gonna fall flat on his face—just like the rest of us.

SANDY: I wish I could believe you, Marie. But you're not the one that's gotta come and pick up the pieces.

MARIE: Marten's got nothing but good intentions.

SANDY: I know all about good intentions.

MARIE: Sandy, you can't keep worrying about what might happen to him. Otherwise you'll be keeping him right where he's at.

SANDY: He's fine right where he's at. So you just tell Eugene to forget it. Now, come on, Marten. Quit your cryin. Me and Marie got some cleaning to do up at Franky's. He's got a visitor coming. And you got some food on the table. So let's go.

SANDY exits. MARTEN stops MARIE.

MARTEN: If I don't get that gun from Eugene—

MARIE: You'll do what?

He pauses.

MARTEN: I'll go to town and get one.

MARIE: Well, you better go set that trap first then.

MARTEN: Oh yeahh. Where's my trap?

He runs to get his trap. He holds it.

And then…SNAP!

He slaps the table.

Lights down.

Scene Three

Friday afternoon. Lights up in the kitchen. FRANK and CLARA have just come in with CLARA's luggage and are kissing passionately. FRANK drops CLARA's bags and gives her a bearhug. CLARA is forced to drop her bags.

FRANK: I could just squeeze you—

CLARA: You are—

FRANK: It's been two whole months. I can't believe—

CLARA: I know, but could you please—Oh Frank!

FRANK: What?

CLARA: It's so beautiful here. And this place is so…

FRANK: What.

CLARA: It's just so…so cute.

FRANK: Oh yeah.

CLARA: I love it here already.

FRANK: Good.

CLARA: We're going to have such a wonderful long weekend, aren't we?

FRANK: Yeah, and—

CLARA: It'll be just like we're camping out.

FRANK: Kind of, I guess—

CLARA: Like we're out in the sticks.

FRANK: Well, we are in the sticks—

CLARA: Just the two of us. Alone. Finally we've got some time together where we can just…talk.

FRANK: Mmm.

CLARA: There won't be any distractions all weekend. We can sit down and figure out all our plans. Like where we're going to live this fall. Maybe we can even check out a place in town. It's so exciting.

            Slight pause.

FRANK: Well, we've gotta do a few other things too.

CLARA: Like what.

FRANK: You've gotta meet my dad.

CLARA: Of course I have to meet him.

FRANK: He applied for that award—

CLARA: That's right. You've already told me that.

FRANK: So I have to get the papers ready.

CLARA: That's fine.

FRANK: And I have to show you that homestead land down at the Ring Field—

CLARA: We can do that tomorrow—

FRANK: You're gonna love it.

CLARA: I'm sure I will, but—right now, we've got some catching up to do.

FRANK: We do?

CLARA: Honey, it's been a whole two months since I've seen you. I can tell you've been working much too hard.

FRANK: You can?

CLARA: You've probably been booked solid in that office—haven't you?

FRANK: Well, yeah—

CLARA: And you've been working on that flood claim and that property dispute and—

FRANK: That hunting case—

CLARA: And who knows what else. But as of right now...

                She kisses him.

                I've got you booked for the whole weekend. And you know something?

                She kisses him.

                Everything's going to be just perfect.

FRANK: Clara.

CLARA: Mmmm?

FRANK: You know something? I couldn't live here without you—

> *She kisses him. She walks him back awkwardly into a chair where she sits on his lap, still kissing.*

> *MARTEN enters. He's wearing a fur cap and fringed coat, and he's clutching a stained burlap bag. He's startled by what he sees. He freezes, not knowing what to do. He wants to back out the door, but he's got a bag to deliver. Just as he ever so quietly goes to set it down, FRANKY sees him.*

Marten!

MARTEN: What?!

FRANK: What are you doing?

MARTEN: Nothing.

FRANK: What do you got there?

MARTEN: Mom said you'd come up to Grandpa's place, so I was just bringing you this.

FRANK: Clara. This is the Kid—

MARTEN: Welcome to the Willows, Clara.

> *He wants to shake hands but fumbles when he has to shift his bag to his other hand.*

CLARA: Thank you…uh…

FRANK: His name is Marten, but we just call him the Kid—

MARTEN: That's me.

FRANK: He lives down the road you came up. In that…hut.

MARTEN: That's my house. You wanna see it?

CLARA: Uh…sure.

MARTEN: It used to be Jim Shingoose's old shack till Alfred bought it for me. That was after Mom's house burned down—

FRANK: You can tell us about that later, OK?

MARTEN: Franky's my buddy.

CLARA: Franky?

FRANK: That's what they call me here.

MARTEN: That's his name—

FRANK: Hey Kid, so how are the chickens?

MARTEN: They're good. The hens are OK, but the cock's a little sick.

FRANK: That's too bad.

MARTEN: Aw, that cock'll be OK once he stops worrying about that mink. So do you want some chickens? Ten bucks a chicken. Mom will pluck em and clean em and I can bring em right over.

FRANK: Yeah…sure.

MARTEN: Chickens ain't dumb, you know. They come in at night. And they scream like hell when that mink comes by. He's just so sneaky. I saw him jump right over my dog one time. I'd shoot him if I had a gun. But Mom won't let me have one. I lost a hundred bucks already cause of that damn mink.

FRANK: You'll get him—

MARTEN: I asked Alfred one time about getting a gun cause he's got a lot of money. But he only gave me some snares. We were shooting coons that day. And he made me dig out their den.

            He gestures throughout.

CLARA: He made you dig out their den?

MARTEN: Yeah, so I dug it out. There were all these coons lined up right next to each other. And then he told me to pull em out.

CLARA: How did you do that?

MARTEN: Well, I just stuck my hand in that den and pulled em out one by one—really fast so they wouldn't bite me. And then I threw em up in the air and when they landed— *(He fires a gun.)* Alfred shot em.

CLARA: He shot those raccoons?

MARTEN: Yep.

FRANK: Did he get em all?

MARTEN: Well, almost. Alfred got real mad when I threw that mom coon up. She was so heavy I couldn't throw her very high—and so she came down too soon and went straight for his leg.

CLARA: So what did he do?

MARTEN: Well, he tried to shoot it, but he missed. And then that coon came after me, so I took off down a rabbit trail.

CLARA: That raccoon was chasing you?

MARTEN: Yeah, she was chasing me and Alfred was yelling "Stop, stop! Chase it back, for chrissake!" So I stopped and turned around and that mom coon went right up on her hind legs snarling at me.

CLARA: So what did you do?

MARTEN: I tried to scare her off. *(He tries scaring the coon.)* But that coon didn't move. So then I picked up a stick and waved it at her. *(He waves the stick.)* And that worked. That mom coon went straight back to Alfred.

CLARA: And then what happened?

MARTEN: Well—he shot her.

CLARA: Oh dear…

MARTEN: Yeah, he got his coon. I never got my gun though.

              He's thinking. He remembers the bag.

              Anyway, that was the day Alfred gave me the snares. That's how come I got this.

              He approaches CLARA with his bag held out. She backs up at first, not sure what he's doing.

              This is for you.

CLARA: Thank you. *(Touched.)*

              She takes the bag, pauses, then peeks inside. She gives a little scream and drops the bag.

FRANK: What?

              FRANK rushes to CLARA.

CLARA: It's a rabbit!

MARTEN: Don't worry, Clara—it's dead.

FRANK: It's all right, Clara.

MARTEN: But I can skin it for you.

CLARA: I'm not used to seeing—

FRANK: Don't worry, I'll take care of it.

MARTEN: Alfred gave me the snares so I could catch some rabbits. Everybody new that comes here gets food.

FRANK: OK, Marten, that's enough—

MARTEN: It'll be good stew, Clara.

CLARA: I really appreciate the…gesture.

MARTEN: How about some chickens? Ten bucks a chicken.

            ALFRED enters.

            I'll kill one for you.

ALFRED: What are you gonna be killing there?

MARTEN: Oh.—Alfred. I was just gonna kill a chicken.

ALFRED: Not inside the house, I hope.

MARTEN: Nooo.

ALFRED: Speaking about chickens, I think I just saw one of
            em running loose down there at your shack.

MARTEN: Really?

ALFRED: Maybe it was that mink.

MARTEN: That mink?

            He rushes out the door—then pops back in.

            Sorry, I gotta go. Bye Clara. *(He bolts.)*

CLARA: Bye Marten.

            MARTEN pops back in.

MARTEN: But I'll come back with a chicken for you.

            He scurries out.

ALFRED: Yeah, you get that chicken before that mink.

FRANK: I thought you were up north till Sunday.

ALFRED: Just got back. Cause you told me I had to be here to
            meet your girl. So this must be her.

FRANK: Dad, this is Clara.

ALFRED: My son says you treat him real well.

CLARA: I try.

ALFRED: We're happy to have you here.

CLARA: Thank you.

ALFRED: And if you need anything, you just call and I'll take care of things. When you meet the ladies up here, they'll tell you this is home. They wouldn't be nowhere else in the whole world. And even if you're from the outside, this is still a damn good place to settle down and raise a family and—

FRANK: Whoa, whoa, whoa. You're running a way ahead of yourself here. It's her first time here, and she's just come through the door—

ALFRED: I'm just telling her that as long as she's part of this family—

FRANK: Dad. Let's slow down here.

CLARA: That's OK, Frank. I really appreciate the welcome— *(To ALFRED.)*

ALFRED: That's good. So anyway, I guess I better be going.

CLARA: You're not leaving already?

ALFRED: Well, you've probably got some things to do—

FRANK: Just a minute now. I've got these papers here.

            He takes out the papers from his briefcase.

ALFRED: What papers.

FRANK: Those application papers—

ALFRED: Now look, son—

FRANK: No, no, no. It's time you got some recognition. All we gotta do is pick up those statements from the neighbours.

ALFRED: Well.

FRANK: Do you see what he's like, Clara? He hates putting himself in the spotlight. To this day I don't know how he's managed to build his business, because he's always out there doing something—

ALFRED: Now come on—

FRANK: And they don't appreciate it. These Métis don't see all the money—

ALFRED: Your girl doesn't need to hear all this—

FRANK: He saved this whole community one time. They tried to send us to some muskeg up north. But he fought that. He told them: "This is our land. And we're not moving." Damn rights. That should be in the history books—

ALFRED: That's enough—

FRANK: He might be worth a lot and have a big house—

ALFRED: Now come on—

FRANK: But it's time he got an award—

ALFRED: Frank—

FRANK: Traditional Ways and Community Service. That's his legacy.

              Pause.

CLARA: I had no idea.

FRANK: He's an important man. Yet to look at him, you'd never know it, would you?

CLARA: Uh, no, I guess—

ALFRED: Now, now. Look, Franky, I was gonna fix that plumbing in the bathroom, but I need them wrenches from the truck. They're behind the seat. Can you get em for me? And then I'll be going.

FRANK: See, he's more concerned about the plumbing than
                about that award.

                FRANK exits.

ALFRED: That boy. I never thought he'd be a lawyer.

CLARA: No?

ALFRED: No. Cause around here, we hate the law. It's
                always worked against us.

CLARA: But isn't that why he went into law? —To try to
                change all that?

ALFRED: I suppose so. But he's been away for just about half
                his life, and he's just been back for a couple of
                months. So whether he can change anything or not
                is something else altogether.

CLARA: Why is that?

ALFRED: Well, you'd have to be around here for a while to
                know what I mean exactly. Now, let me explain
                something. The law has always tried to clamp
                down on us, so it's kinda like…he's joined the
                enemy. We got everything we need here.

CLARA: I can see why he wants to be back.

ALFRED: That's right, and he's the only one of my kids who's
                come back.

CLARA: I hope you win that award.

ALFRED: I know Franky wants to get those statements, but
                he shouldn't be leaving you alone just yet. Once he
                gets something into his head—

CLARA: No, it's important. Why don't you go out with
                Frank right now, and I'll get unpacked—

                FRANK enters with a gun.

FRANK: I couldn't find those wrenches back there, but I found Grampa's old gun.

ALFRED: That's the one.

FRANK: I haven't seen it since I was a kid. This gun, Clara, is what Grampa used to shoot moose with.

ALFRED: He saved your Uncle Johnny's life with that gun. Isn't that right?

FRANK: Uh…yeah—

ALFRED: That's right. They were out with an American hunter one time—and that guy wounded a bear, and it took off on him. So Johnny comes along and goes down on all fours trying to track that bear and damned if that bear doesn't come charging through a clump of willows right at Uncle Johnny. Well, Grampa pulls out that gun and tells him to "Git down there!" just as he took a shot at that bear, right over Johnny's head, and that bear fell dead— right down in front of Johnny. That night Johnny went out and got drunk and never came home for three days. And after that he started going to church.

FRANK: This is the gun that Grampa died with.

ALFRED: Yeah, that's right. And I was the one that came across him.

                He was lying in the snow as if he'd just laid down for his afternoon nap. He was under that pine tree, the one that looks out over Alfred Lake.

                He said he'd be out on the trapline that day, and so I followed his tracks, right to where he was lying.

                The day before—he told me I could have his gun. And I didn't know what he meant. He knew he was gonna be passing on.

Pause. FRANK hands the gun over to ALFRED.

FRANK: If that gun could tell stories, it'd be in a museum. *(To CLARA.)*

ALFRED hands the gun back to FRANK.

ALFRED: But until then, this gun is yours.

FRANK: Mine?

ALFRED: That's for coming home. All of his brothers and sisters and most of his cousins have left. And they won't be back. That's why it's important for him to be here. *(To CLARA.)* And for you, too.

CLARA: Me?

ALFRED: This community needs some new blood. It can't be allowed to just die out without a bang—

EUGENE: *(EUGENE comes banging through the door with a dirty sack of potatoes. He's sweaty and dirty after a day of clearing trees.)* I brought you these potatoes like you wanted. Marie told me to bring em by yesterday, so I threw em in the back of the truck and then forgot all about em. So that's why I'm here.

FRANK: Well, that's good—

EUGENE: The new ones ain't ready yet–

He rummages for a potato to show FRANK, dirt coming off the sack. More dirt falls as he takes out the potato.

—but these ones are still fine—

ALFRED: Do you think you could spread any more of that dirt around the house?

EUGENE: What do you mean?

ALFRED: I mean, you're throwing it around like an old dog who's just had a good roll—

EUGENE: I'm sorry, Alfred, I didn't know you were allergic to dirt. I guess I'll have to go for a dip in your lake. Or would that be called trespassing?

ALFRED: Trespassing—

EUGENE: I seen someone digging around in my garden last week. He was digging up a couple of hills. They weren't ready yet, but he was sure looking.

ALFRED: There's nothing like a few new potatoes. He musta been checkin em out.

FRANK: Thanks for the potatoes—

EUGENE: No problem. You come down to my garden any time and dig yourself a couple of hills. A little bit of deer meat, some bannock, a potato or two, and it makes you wonder what the rich are doing.

FRANK: I needed some for the weekend. My girlfriend—

EUGENE: You must be Clara.

CLARA: Yes, I am—

EUGENE: Well, I'm Eugene. My wife Marie says she'd like to meet you.

CLARA: By all means—

ALFRED: I'm on my way. When you're finished here, I'll be down at the fur shack. Clara says she won't miss you for a little while.

CLARA: No, I won't.

ALFRED: By the way, Eugene. When are you ever gonna get that bell up on the church? I promised the priest it'd be up this spring.

EUGENE: It'll be up there.

ALFRED: I think I already paid you for the job.

EUGENE: That bell will be calling the sinners before you can say "Jesus Christ come down and save my dirty soul."

ALFRED: You wouldn't know a prayer if it came down from heaven and struck you blind.

EUGENE: I might go blind, but at least I'd still hear that bell chiming, wouldn't I?

ALFRED: What in the hell are you talking about? Achh.

FRANK: I'll meet you down there.

                ALFRED exits, kicking a dirt lump as he goes.

EUGENE: Sorry about the dirt—

FRANK: Don't worry about it.

EUGENE: I was just wondering if I could get a cheque from you. I just finished clearing them trees at the Ring Field—

FRANK: Yeah, I can pay you.

EUGENE: And what about Marie's cheque? She was gonna pick it up, but I can take it off your hands—

FRANK: I got them both here.

EUGENE: Yeah, you got a really nice spot there down at the Ring Field, looking out over your dad's lake.

FRANK: It's not actually his lake.

EUGENE: Yeah, but it's named after him. Not just anyone's got connections to the Department of Natural Resources.

FRANK: Here are the cheques.

EUGENE: If you need any more help—

FRANK: Have a good weekend, Eugene.

EUGENE: I'm not doing nothing this weekend.

               He's at the door, ready to go out.

               Unless, uh…hey, do you need any meat?

FRANK: Actually, the freezer's empty—

EUGENE: Yeah? I bet you Clara's never had any deer meat neither—

MARIE: *(MARIE enters, rushing in.)* Eugene—

EUGENE: Hey, Marie. I was just talking about getting a deer—

MARIE: Eugene. The game wardens are here.

EUGENE: The game wardens?

MARIE: They found a deer.

EUGENE: Where.

MARIE: I just left the house to find you.

EUGENE: Are all the kids there?

MARIE: I told them to lock up and I'd call when I found you.

EUGENE: We gotta call em then.

FRANK: Here's the phone.

MARIE: Frank.

FRANK: What?—

EUGENE: Where'd they find the deer?

MARIE: Down at the Ring Field.

FRANK: At the Ring Field?

EUGENE: I was just down there. I been there all week.

MARIE: Down behind the willows. Right by those round bales of alfalfa.

EUGENE: Well, that's Franky's land.

MARIE: They found the deer on your land, Franky.

FRANK: I never shot it.

MARIE: They just took the horns.

FRANK: Jesus, what the—

CLARA: What does that mean?

FRANK: It means they're gonna be looking for me.

CLARA: For what?

EUGENE: For poaching.

CLARA: Poaching?

FRANK: I could be charged.

MARIE: He could lose his licence to practice.

> *EUGENE is on the phone to his kids. CLARA goes to FRANK.*

EUGENE: Jimmy, now you listen to me. Those game wardens can't come in and search the house without an adult there. Now we're all gonna be at the Kid's shack...No, they won't be coming around there, and we'll be able to see the house from that shack. Now, what you and Amy gotta do is stoke that fire real good. And then you go into the freezer and you get that meat—that's right, you gotta take it all cause that's what they're looking for. And then you gotta take that meat and throw it in the fire... No no, not all at once. Don't put too much in at one time cause otherwise you'll smother that fire. Now, that meat's gonna take all...that's right...it's gonna take all night to burn, so you and Amy are gonna have to stay up and keep throwing it in. The other kids you're gonna have to put them in the back bedroom...they'll be fine. Just tell em we can't be there. OK? Now, when you're all done burning that meat, you can open up them curtains in the kitchen...that's right, and you keep em closed. And when you're done, you pull that flour sack offa the curtain rod. We'll see it from the Kid's shack, and then we'll know it's OK to come home... Yeah, them game wardens are gonna be around all night waiting for me. No, don't open the door for them. You just do exactly what I said. Me and your Mom are gonna be watching you from the shack. *(He hangs up.)* Jesus christ.

MARIE: Everything's gonna be all right. *(To CLARA.)* But you're just gonna have to stay here on your own.

FRANK: I'm gonna have to stay with her—

MARIE: No, you'll be leaving with us. You can't stay here cause they'll be coming around for you.

FRANK: I'm gonna have to see my dad. He's gotta get rid of his meat.

EUGENE: Well, come on then, we gotta go.

MARIE: You keep the doors locked, and don't turn on the lights when it gets dark. They'll be coming by, so just make sure you don't answer the door. After dark, maybe Franky can sneak back up.

CLARA: I'll be fine.

FRANK: Are you sure?

CLARA: Don't get caught.

          EUGENE and MARIE exit. MARIE stands by the door..

MARIE: I'm Marie. We'll have coffee tomorrow, OK?

CLARA: OK—

FRANK: Clara, I'm sorry about—

CLARA: We'll talk later. Now, go catch up to them. *(She kisses him.)*

FRANK: I'll see you tonight.

             He exits.

             CLARA moves away from the door. Pauses. Goes back and locks it.

             Lights down.

Scene Four

             Low lights come up on MARTEN's shack where EUGENE is at the window with MARIE peering out behind him. MARTEN is sitting as far away as possible from the door, working on a new slingshot, worried about the game wardens coming. SANDY is checking through MARTEN's willows.

EUGENE: Jimmy's got that fire stoked and Amy's probably in the back bedroom trying to keep the girls from being scared. There's no reason why my kids gotta be scared all the time by those goddamn game wardens. Every year. Every year they gotta come and do this same goddamn thing to us. Jesus christ, you shouldn't have to be scared to provide for your own family. We're Métis, for chrissake, and we know more about this bush than they do. We've always been living on this land.

MARIE: Now calm down, Eugene. You're scaring the Kid—

             EUGENE moves away from the window and MARIE takes his place.

EUGENE: Calm down? How in the hell are we gonna eat this winter if I get charged? And sure as hell they're gonna blame me for shooting that deer.

SANDY: Well, they should know you wouldn't leave a deer out there. You wouldn't kill it just for the horns.

EUGENE: No, I wouldn't.

SANDY: If it comes down to it, I'll take the charge for it.

EUGENE: No, you're not taking any charge.

SANDY: It must of been one of those guys from town.

EUGENE: It's on Franky's land. And if they don't get me, they're gonna get Franky.

MARTEN: But Franky's a lawyer.

MARIE: He won't be fighting in court if he gets charged. He'll likely lose his licence.

SANDY: You don't think Franky shot it.

EUGENE: I'm the one that taught Franky how to hunt. He'd never do that. He wouldn't waste the hind end off a skunk.

MARIE: But they're gonna be looking for him.

MARTEN: Franky's gonna get in trouble?

EUGENE: He'd lose that woman of his most likely and probably go to jail. And you can't practice law in jail. No, and they'd probably take his guns, too.

MARTEN: His guns?

EUGENE: They got Norbert and Horace's guns last year. And if you got charged, Kid, and you had a gun, they'd take it away for sure.

SANDY: He's not gonna own a gun, so stop putting ideas in his head.

EUGENE: What do you mean he's not gonna own a gun? I've got one promised to him—as soon as he brings me the cash.

SANDY: You should know better. You were the one that took him out last year—"Just to shoot a few coyotes," you said.

EUGENE: That's right.

SANDY: But I bet you didn't count on him just about shooting Alfred down there on the Lake Road.

EUGENE: He didn't know Alfred was behind that rise—

SANDY: I can still hear Alfred—"What a stupid fucken thing to do to take that boy hunting"—

EUGENE: Someone's gotta take him out—

SANDY: And now you wanna sell him a gun?

EUGENE: He needs one to take care of himself. God knows no one else does.

                 SANDY slaps a willow on the table.

SANDY: Don't you goddamn well say that. I'm down here feeding my boy every day. And you know as well as I do the only reason he's down here is because he burned down my house two years ago. I'll be taking him back—once I get the Murdock place next year.

EUGENE: And where are you gonna get the money—

SANDY: He won't be burning down that place cause there ain't no wood stove there.

MARIE: It wasn't the Kid's fault, Sandy. You need to have something behind the stove to protect the wall. That boy's not dumb. You gotta let him be a man.

EUGENE: Yeah, and you shouldn't be letting him move back in with you. He's fine right where he is.

SANDY: Bullshit. You're not down here every day. If he had
              a father, maybe it'd be different. I came down here
              last winter and the water was frozen on the stove.
              And there was frost on the walls. He had no
              firewood cause his axe was broken. And he didn't
              know enough to borrow one from you, Eugene.
              And you want him to have a gun.

MARTEN: It wasn't cause my axe was broken—I was sick.

SANDY: The only reason I'm saying all this is cause I love
              that boy. And I don't wanna see him hurt.

EUGENE: But he's gotta be able to look after himself. Like my
              kids down there. I'm not there, but they're just
              keeping that chimney smoking—Now what are
              those game wardens up to.

MARIE: They've probably been to Franky's by now, so he's
              likely over there helping Alfred burn his meat.

SANDY: I'll say one thing: no one shoots a deer without
              someone else knowing about it.

MARIE: Someone must have heard a shot, or seen someone
              leaving that field.

EUGENE: That's not always the case. Some of us can slip in
              and out without no one seeing a thing. You know
              that yourself, Marie. Even the Kid would know
              something like that.

MARTEN: Me?

EUGENE: (EUGENE turns and studies MARTEN.) Why, do
              you know something about that deer?

MARIE: Leave the Kid out of it.

SANDY: If my son had seen anything, he'd tell me.
              Wouldn't you?

              He's keeping busy with his slingshot. Just then,
              headlights light up the window.

MARIE: There's someone coming.

MARTEN: The game wardens?

EUGENE: I can't believe they'd come looking for you, Kid.

MARTEN: Looking for me?

EUGENE: You got nothing in here but a little rabbit meat—

                MARTEN runs out the door.

                He's acting like he shot the damn deer.

SANDY: You didn't have to scare him like that.

MARIE: It's only Jake Munson. He must of picked up his bales.

SANDY: Well, are you gonna go find him?

EUGENE: He'll be back. He's likely out there checking on those birds. Waiting for his mink, I bet.

                Lights fade. Music.

Scene Five

Low light in the dark kitchen. CLARA faces the door, having heard something outside. She's startled by a sudden knocking. She presses her back against the door, arms extended as a barricade. She slides down the door when the knocking continues. She waits, and when the knocking comes, she reaches for the gun propped by the door. She cradles the gun as the light fades.

Scene Six

> *The fur shack. A knock. Lights up as ALFRED sets his bottle on the table. FRANKY is looking out the window.*

ALFRED: I don't need to burn my meat.

FRANK: Yes, you do. They're checking everybody's.

ALFRED: They know my meat's all got tags from last season. Now, come on over and have a drink.

FRANK: Maybe you got nothing to worry about, but me? That damn deer was shot on my land.

ALFRED: You already told me that.

FRANK: Look, Dad. I don't know if you realize, but if I'm charged for this—

ALFRED: Yes, I know you'll lose your licence—

FRANK: And how do you think that's gonna look in the community. The only lawyer these Métis got and he's in goddamn jail. And on top of that, I won't be building any house. And without that house, I'll have no wife. And without my wife, I'll have nothing.

ALFRED: I wouldn't worry about her too much.

FRANK: Now what's that supposed to mean?

ALFRED: Well—the women up here know this place—

FRANK: And Clara will get to know it too—

ALFRED: Just like that goddamn Sandy.

FRANK: That goddamn Sandy?—

ALFRED: Yes, that goddamn Sandy. She's from the same place as that girl of yours. She belongs to the same people who wouldn't buy my wood when I was starting out. If you remember, and I suppose you wouldn't cause you were too young, I had to go all the way—

FRANK: You had to go all the way to Prince Albert—

ALFRED: That's right. To sell my timber.

FRANK: Clara doesn't even come from the city. She's from Invermere.

ALFRED: Where those Scotch come from? Those pure blood Scotch are all the same. Look at Sandy. Once they move in, they think they own it all.

FRANK: Sandy doesn't own a thing.

ALFRED: They took your grandfather's land when he couldn't pay his taxes. And you watch—that girl of yours will be digging in your wallet—

FRANK: You don't even know her.

ALFRED: No, but I do know you'd be happier with one of the local girls. What's wrong with them?

FRANK: The local girls?

ALFRED: Like that Marie. You two had something going one time. Whatever happened to that?

FRANK: You sent me away to school in Saskatoon—

ALFRED: Well, after your mother passed away—

FRANK: For five years.

ALFRED: Yeah, but you coulda come back and married that Marie.

FRANK: Dad, I was at university and then I went to law school. Besides she ended up with Eugene.

ALFRED: Yes, I know she went for that sonuvabitch. And if

there's anyone that shot that deer, I'm telling you it'd be him.

FRANK: Who?—Eugene?

ALFRED: Someone should pick up the phone and turn that black bastard in.

FRANK: You can't be serious. Eugene wouldn't just take the horns. You know that better than anybody. No one does that down here.

ALFRED: Just hold on there. I remember last year when he shot that moose down at Dry Lake. I was coming back from the trapline. And there was Eugene cutting off the horns with a hack saw. I thought he was gonna take that meat home. But it wasn't two days later he was at my door looking for a bit of meat. And I saw that carcass out there—maybe not all of it—but most of it was still there—wasted.

FRANK: He couldn't have done that.

ALFRED: You don't know Eugene any more. Why, he's at my door every other week looking for a handout. You watch, he'll be at your door the same way. If it's not a case of beer, he wants me to write him a cheque— so he can pay his fucken Hydro.

FRANK: I know he's like that with money, but I've never known him to waste an animal.

ALFRED: If you knew what you were doing, you'd phone them game wardens and tell em to check him out. I know he's got them horns stashed somewhere.

FRANK: I don't care if he did or not, I couldn't turn in one of my own friends.

ALFRED: Do you want to be a lawyer or not? Someone's gonna have to do it. Otherwise—you're gonna get charged.

Slight pause.

FRANK: I know. *(Troubled, he goes to leave.)*

ALFRED: That's right. You just do what you gotta do.

FRANK turns and looks at him.

If you don't have the guts to make that call...

FRANK exits.

After a moment, ALFRED looks up at the antlers. He takes them down as the music comes up and fades.

Scene Seven

Next day. Saturday morning. CLARA is sitting at the table. FRANK comes in, buttoning up his shirt.

FRANK: What's the gun doing over here?

CLARA: You got back so late, and I was scared.

FRANK: Scared of what?

CLARA: The game wardens were here. They kept banging on the door.

FRANK: What were you gonna do? Shoot them?

CLARA: They kept knocking.

FRANK: So you picked up the gun.

CLARA: They kept calling your name.

FRANK: You didn't let them in?

CLARA: No, I didn't. But I wanted to tell them you didn't do it. Frank, you've gotta call them.

FRANK: Are you crazy? You don't go calling the game wardens.

CLARA: You didn't do it, and they're going to come back anyway.

FRANK: Well, let them. I've got nothing to hide.

CLARA: They'll probably just want to tell you they found the deer on your land.

FRANK: They'll charge the first person they find.

CLARA: In that case, you better find out who shot that deer.

FRANK: I've got other things to do.

CLARA: Well, who do you think shot it then?

FRANK: I've got nothing to do with it.

CLARA: You mean, you know who shot it?

FRANK: I've gotta get those papers signed for my dad, and then we're gonna go see that land.

CLARA: I'm not going anywhere until you deal with this.

FRANK: They'll find him without me.

CLARA: You have an obligation to me too, don't forget. Now, who did it?

FRANK: I'm not turning in a friend.

CLARA: Who? You mean, Eugene?

FRANK: I'm not saying it was him, but Dad said he probably did it.

CLARA: Well, he was clearing your land all week, wasn't he?

FRANK: Yes.

CLARA: And he does shoot deer, doesn't he?

FRANK: Yes, but he takes the whole animal. Now, will you please just get off my back!

CLARA: What, do you want me to leave already?

              EUGENE enters.

              Look, it's either you or Eugene!—

              CLARA looks at him for just a moment. She can't stay now, but she has to step past EUGENE who's blocking the door.

              Excuse me. (*Without meeting his eye.*)

              He pauses first before letting her by.

EUGENE: What, is she feeling guilty?

FRANK: For what?

EUGENE: Someone phoned the game wardens on me.

FRANK: Are you accusing her?

EUGENE: Well, was she accusing me?

FRANK: She wouldn't phone anyone unless I told her to.

EUGENE: So then you told her to.

FRANK: I never told her anything.

EUGENE: Well, they said someone reported me, and now they want me to go in. They said it was a .30-30— just like this one here.

FRANK: Are you accusing me now?

EUGENE: You own a .30-30, and it's your land.

FRANK: I think there's a better chance you shot it. I hear you're in the habit of shooting for horns.

EUGENE: You asshole. You know well enough I'd never do that.

FRANK: I heard about you down at Dry Lake last year. You shot a moose and took the horns.

EUGENE: Where'd you hear that horseshit? I'm sick and tired of being accused for everything around here. Munson's dog gets run over last week and now Munson's accusing me. He says he's gonna come over and shoot my dog. I can't believe I'd hear those lies coming from you. Who'd you get your information from anyway?

FRANK: What's it matter? The point is—

EUGENE: The point is, I think you heard it from your dad, that sonuvabitch.

FRANK: Maybe I did—but he's never lied to me before.

EUGENE: Bullshit. Now, you listen to me. I took every piece of meat that was on that moose, and I left the guts and the hide—and I even left the horns. If you want proof, I can take you right back to the very spot and those horns will still be there.

FRANK: You know you can't get in there at this time of year.

EUGENE: You're just like the rest of em, aren't you— including your dad—applying for an award—

FRANK: You and Marie wouldn't even have a house if it wasn't for my dad—

EUGENE: If it wasn't for your dad, I'd be far better off. Who do you think has made all his money for him?

FRANK: Get out.

EUGENE: What, are you gonna throw me out then?

FRANK steps toward him. EUGENE clenches a fist.

Yeah, wouldn't that look good in court—me accused of assaulting a lawyer. Who do you think they'd believe?

He pokes FRANK on the chest. Slight pause.

FRANK steps back.

FRANK: Look, Eugene—

EUGENE: Now you look. They're gonna try and throw me in jail. And they goddamn will, if I have to go to legal aid. They think we're all guilty until proven innocent. They don't care if we go to jail, for chrissake.

FRANK: I don't wanna see that—

EUGENE: And to think that I came over here to get the only lawyer we got. The guy I want defending me is now accusing me. You think I killed that deer.

FRANK: I don't know who—

EUGENE: You're no better than that McDiarmid and the rest of them lawyers. What did you come back here for, anyway? To pick up where your dad left off?

FRANK: What?

EUGENE: You've taken his word over mine. There's your .30-30. You better put it away.

            EUGENE exits. FRANK picks up the gun. He holds it for a moment then puts it up in the gunrack.

            Short blackout, 2-3 seconds.

Scene Eight

            Late Saturday morning. Immediate sound of a leghold trap snapping shut. A yell. Lights up on MARTEN's shack. CLARA is standing outside the shack, peering in, wanting to go in but not sure. MARTEN is banging the table, hunched over, trying to remove a leghold trap from his thumb. There's a lot of blood on his hands, and some on the table. CLARA rushes in.

MARTEN: That mink!—

CLARA: Marten! What's wrong?—

MARTEN: He got away!—

CLARA: Where is it?—

MARTEN: Arhhh!—I can't get it off!—

CLARA: You're bleeding all over!—

MARTEN: Just get it off me—

CLARA: Where?—

MARTEN: Just push here—

CLARA: Push where?—

MARTEN: Right here—

CLARA: There's blood right there—

MARTEN: It's just my blood—

CLARA: OK, OK, hold on—

MARTEN: I am, I am, it's caught.

> *CLARA pushes on the tail of the trap, but it slips, and then slides a few inches along the table, wrenching his thumb. He shouts again.*

            Arhhh!—

CLARA: I'm sorry!—

MARTEN: Just push down on it, Clara. Push down on it!

CLARA: OK, I will, I will.

> *She releases his thumb. MARTEN grabs his thumb and jumps up and down.*

MARTEN: Ow ow ow ow—

CLARA: Let me see it—

MARTEN: It's OK—

CLARA: No, you've got to let me take a look at it. Maybe you'll need stitches—

MARTEN: No no no, I don't need no stitches—

CLARA: Marten, you're going to bleed to death—

MARTEN: OK then, hurry.

              He relents and holds out his thumb—at a distance, not wanting to look at it.

CLARA: Oh my, you're going to need some bandages and a little antiseptic.

MARTEN: Auntie who?

CLARA: Anti-septic.

MARTEN: Oh.

              CLARA looks around, realizing the futility of finding anything in the shack.

CLARA: Do you have any clean water?

MARTEN: No, but there's some tea right there.

CLARA: You can't use tea.

MARTEN: No?

CLARA: Do you have any clean rags, at least?

              He stops to think about it then remembers his underwear drying on the binder twine clothesline inside the shack.

MARTEN: There's my underwear. They're clean, but it's my only pair.

CLARA: That's the only clean thing you've got?

MARTEN: Yeah, cause I don't do my socks till Sunday.

CLARA: It'll have to do then.

            She grabs the underwear from the line and rips it in half.

MARTEN: Wait, what are you doing? I got no underwear now.

CLARA: Just give me your hand. I'll get you a pair from Frank.

            She wraps his thumb.

            This'll stop it for now. There.

MARTEN: Thanks, Clara. You're sure a good doctor.

CLARA: Now exactly what happened in here?

MARTEN: That mink got away last night— but I got its toe. See?

            He holds up the mink's toe.

CLARA: Very nice.

MARTEN: I just came back in to set that trap again. And that's when—

CLARA: You got caught in your own trap.

MARTEN: Last time I caught my finger.

            He points to the scar.

CLARA: You really do need a first aid kit. You don't have anything in here.

            He looks around the shack, perplexed.

MARTEN: I got lots of stuff in here. Like this here splint.

            He points to a stick—still holding his thumb.

We put that on Eugene's dog—after he got finished chasing Oscar Franson's snowmobile. That old dog got run right over. But we fixed him up. See, I got lots of things here. Like that old seat there. That comes from Franky's first truck. I got that after we got his truck outta the ravine.

CLARA: How'd it get there?

MARTEN: Franky was teaching me how to drive. And this here picture of the deer comes from Marie. She was getting her deer licence one time so Eugene could get another deer. And she stole that picture right outta the game warden's office.

CLARA: What about this old...animal?

MARTEN: Well, Mom caught that mink.

CLARA: How'd she catch it?

MARTEN: She caught it in her cooler. It was in there after the sardines. So she just shut the lid and locked it up. But that mink musta gone crazy inside there, just a flippin and a floppin away—that cooler was dancing around so much she couldn't open it up. So she just filled it full of holes with her .22 until that mink stopped moving. And then she stuffed it for me.

CLARA: Really.

MARTEN: And I still got the cooler too. See, it's still full of holes.

            He points toward the corner at an old blue Coleman cooler full of bullet holes. A set of broken deer antlers sits on the cooler.

CLARA: I can see that.

MARTEN: And them antlers I got from Mom. She was just a girl when she shot it.

MARTEN sets the antlers on the table.

CLARA:	She was just a girl?
MARTEN:	Yeah. That's when she was with my dad.
CLARA:	When she was a girl?
MARTEN:	Yeah. But he broke them antlers before he died.
CLARA:	When did he die?
MARTEN:	Well, I thought he was dead one time.
CLARA:	Uh huh…
MARTEN:	But now he's not.
CLARA:	Oh. You thought he was dead one time…
MARTEN:	But now he's not. Do you have a dad?
CLARA:	I do, but I haven't seen him in a long time. He left when I was twelve.
MARTEN:	That's too bad. But you still got a mom, don't you?
CLARA:	Yeah, I do, but—she was sick for quite a while—and then she got married again.
MARTEN:	That's good.
CLARA:	Not really. They…sort of forgot about me after they got married.
MARTEN:	Ohh. So you were all alone.
CLARA:	Yeah, I don't want that to happen again.
MARTEN:	What?
CLARA:	Losing someone you love.
MARTEN:	Who?
CLARA:	First my dad—and then my mom.

MARTEN: No. That's why you need Franky, right?

CLARA: That's right.

MARTEN: You're gonna get married and have a family.

CLARA: Well—

MARTEN: And live right here in the Willows.

CLARA: Maybe in town, but—

MARTEN: I need Franky cause he's gonna take me hunting.

CLARA: Yes, but there won't be any hunting if he gets charged.

MARTEN: No?

CLARA: We've got to find out who did it, Marten.

        MARTEN looks at the antlers.

        I don't know. Maybe it was Eugene.

MARTEN: Eugene? I know it wasn't Eugene.

CLARA: How do you know that?

MARTEN: I mean, Eugene wouldn't do that.

CLARA: Well, somebody did. And if he doesn't come forward and tell the truth, then Frank's going to go to jail.

MARTEN: But if they take Eugene, who's gonna look after them kids? They're gonna go hungry.

CLARA: It's not a very good situation, but you've got to do what's right—even if it means making a sacrifice.

MARTEN: What do you mean?

        She points her finger emphatically.

CLARA: It means giving yourself up and telling the truth—

MARTEN: I don't have to give myself up to no one!

CLARA: I'm not talking about you—

MARTEN: Just stop it and leave me alone!

            He runs out, accidentally knocking the trap to the floor. CLARA goes to follow MARTEN but stops. She picks up the trap. MARIE and SANDY, with MARTEN in tow, enter.

SANDY: What the hell you been doing to my kid? He's got blood all over him and he's scared all to hell. What were you making him do?

CLARA: I wasn't making him—

SANDY: Bullshit. You musta done something. And what in the fuck you doing in my son's place anyway?

CLARA: I just came in—

MARTEN: But Mom—

SANDY: Look, you little bitch, I don't know what you're fucken up to, but if you touch my son again, I'll shoot you like a goddamn dog on the run. I seen this shit before, and so help me god, if you've laid a finger on him I'll kick your ass all the way back to the city—

MARIE: Whoa whoa whoa Sandy. Let's find out what happened first.

SANDY: Yah, so what the fuck happened then?

CLARA: He caught his thumb in the trap, and I was only trying to help—

            She sets the trap down.

SANDY: My son doesn't bolt from his own place if someone's trying to help him.

CLARA: Look, we were just talking and he...and he
            snapped.

SANDY: Snapped? He doesn't snap for no reason. You must
            of said something.

MARIE: What did you tell him?

CLARA: I just told him he wasn't going hunting if Frank
            gets charged.

SANDY: He's not going hunting anyway—

MARTEN: Yes, I am—

SANDY: You be quiet.

MARIE: Is that what made him run?

CLARA: I was just telling him that whoever did it has got to
            turn himself in.

MARIE: You're right, but they don't turn themselves in
            around here.

SANDY: Yah, this isn't the city. Where do you think you are
            anyways?

MARIE: Something else must have scared him. What else
            did you say?

CLARA: I'm worried about Frank.

MARIE: Yeah?

CLARA: I just came here to see Frank. We were supposed to
            have a quiet long weekend and—

SANDY: What did you tell him?

CLARA: I don't know—

SANDY: What did you fucken tell him?

MARTEN: I told her Eugene wouldn't do it.

MARIE: Eugene? What kind of lies are you telling him?

CLARA: I just heard Eugene might have done it and Frank—

MARIE: Frank told you that?

CLARA: He didn't know for sure—

MARIE: Frank doesn't know shit.

SANDY: And Marie should know. God knows she spent enough time with him.

MARIE: Where'd he get it from?

SANDY: He got it from Alfred, didn't he?

CLARA: Well, Alfred told him—

SANDY: That lying bastard. Don't you believe a word he says! He'd sell his own kids if he knew he could make a dollar. And Frank's just fooling himself if he thinks he can trust his dad. I know all about his dad, and believe me, if I told you, you'd think twice about marrying that boy. I came in here from the outside—just like you're doing. So let me tell you something about this community. You marry the Métis, you marry the dead. All this bullshit about Métis culture and Métis pride—that's just a cover-up. This place is sick. You'll get eaten alive out here. If you think you can dance your pretty little ass in here and settle down with a Métis—

MARIE: Wait a minute, Sandy. We got problems, yeah— but we're not all like that. In fact, you're more Métis than most of us—

SANDY: Well, Franky might think he knows this place—

MARIE: She's right about Franky—

SANDY: Damn rights. He might of been in the city getting himself an education—and he might think he can parade back in here and "save his people" but he'll turn out just like the rest of em. Once he's got you trapped, there's no way out. He'll tell you he loves you, but you wait—that'll change.

ALFRED appears at the door.

SANDY: Alfred doesn't take second place to no one—and that includes you—

ALFRED: Looks like we're having a meeting here. So what's on the agenda?

SANDY: What'd you come down here for?

ALFRED: I just come down to tell Clara that Franky's not in trouble.

Slight pause.

And he wants you up at the house. Says he's ready to show you that land.

CLARA: What do you mean Frank's not in trouble?

ALFRED: Now you run along there. He's been driving around looking for you. He's been worried.

Slight pause.

CLARA: I guess I better go, but I'll have you up for coffee in the morning.

SANDY: If you say so.

MARIE: No no, we'll be there.

CLARA: And I'm really sorry for—

SANDY: Just save it, all right.

CLARA looks at the two of them, MARTEN, and then exits. ALFRED watches her leave.

ALFRED: Well, that's about all I came for—

He goes to leave.

MARIE: If Franky's not in trouble, then someone else is.

ALFRED: You're right—they got the guy.

SANDY: What've you done, Alfred?

MARIE: Who do they have?

ALFRED: They got Eugene. He's down at Natural Resources.

MARIE: I know what you told Franky. And that's what you told the game wardens.

ALFRED: Eugene's got a history of taking what he wants.

SANDY: That's bullshit. He keeps most of us fed all winter.

MARIE: Last year it was Horace Leclair. And the year before that it was Norbert Houle. And now it's Eugene. You use all of us for what you want, and it's gonna come back on you, Alfred. You wouldn't be doing all this if you didn't have something to do with it. I know what you've done.

SANDY: Exactly. You've always made us pay.

ALFRED: I think it's the other way around. I've been the bank around here. Now you take that Murdock place you want.

SANDY: What about it?

ALFRED: I got my eye on that place too. And unless you think you can outbid me—I suggest you just sit there and be quiet. You had that old place of yours burnt down by that kid of yours. And last year he froze his foot and you weren't around. And before that, if you remember, he just about shot me. I didn't say nothing about that. But all that can change.

SANDY: What are you saying?

ALFRED: I'm saying your son can be taken away and put in a
              home. So before you start opening your mouth and
              telling me what I know and don't know, you better
              think about it.

MARIE: That's enough—

ALFRED: And the same goes for you. *(To MARIE.)* Don't you
              forget who owns most of the land around here.
              And if you own the land, goddamnit, you own the
              people. Nobody works up here unless I say so.
              Haven't you learned that yet? Eugene's gonna
              have work all winter, and I'll find you work up at
              the house. Now you think about that offer.
              Otherwise it's gonna be a long winter for those kids
              of yours.

                   Slight pause.

              And as for you. *(To MARTEN.)* In a couple of
              months, you're gonna be chopping wood and
              killing those chickens. I seen Peter Allbright's got
              axes on sale. Now you go on and get in the truck,
              and we'll go up and get you one of them axes.
              Come on.

                   MARTEN looks at SANDY.

SANDY: He doesn't need your handouts.

ALFRED: You get in the truck.

SANDY: Marten.

                   *ALFRED takes MARTEN's axe. It's dull, rusted
                   and taped up with black electrical tape a foot from
                   the handle. He waggles it at SANDY.*

ALFRED: Is this what he's been using? He'll kill himself with
              this. Is that what you want?

                   SANDY turns away.

              Come on. Get in that truck.

Slight pause. MARTEN exits. ALFRED follows.
MARIE watches them out as she speaks. SANDY
will sit down on the cooler, the fight gone out of her.

MARIE: This is exactly what happened two winters ago. Eugene turned Alfred in for throwing his chemical pails into the creek, you remember that. Eugene went right up to his door and told him: "That creek feeds into your goddamn lake, and we eat that fish. You're poisoning your own lake, for chrissake." So when Alfred got fined, he cut him out. And that winter my kids were living on lard and pickle sandwiches. They were eating boiled beaver by December. And if it wasn't for your kid and those chickens that's about all we woulda had. Isn't that right.

SANDY: He can't take my kid.

MARIE: We've been poor before, and we can be poor again.

SANDY: They'll take him all the way to Saskatoon, and I'll never see him there. I got no way of getting in and outta there. He doesn't belong there—he belongs in the bush. Right here. It's the only place he knows. He's my kid, for chrissake.

MARIE: That man is out of control.

                SANDY stands.

SANDY: But you know what, Marie? I'm putting a stop to this right now. You keep telling me that all I do is talk. Well, you watch. I'm gonna go after what he loves most.

MARIE: And what's that?

SANDY: That boy of his. Alfred's got plans for him. Franky doesn't know it, but you can bet he's getting it all. That boy's gonna own the whole operation. And that's why Franky got that land so cheap. And that's why Alfred wants him back. He's got no one else.

MARIE: But Franky's come back for other reasons.

SANDY: Once I'm through with him, he'll wish he'd never come back. I'm telling you right now that boy's not staying here. And neither's that little bitch of his. She'll have nothing to do with him once I'm done with her.

MARIE: Listen, Sandy—

SANDY: He wants to take my kid. Well, I'm going after his.

MARIE: What you're telling me is that you're gonna stop Alfred by wrecking Franky's life.

SANDY: I won't be wrecking his life—I'll be saving him.

MARIE: Saving him from what?

SANDY: From his dad, who do you think?

MARIE: What about Clara? She's got nothing to do with it. You'd be destroying her too—just to get back at Alfred.

SANDY: Why would I care about her? She's coming in here like a little princess.

MARIE: Look, Sandy. I know we can't let things go on like this. But the way you're going about it is wrong.

SANDY: I don't have a choice anymore. When it comes to Alfred, there's nothing wrong about it. It has to be done.

MARIE: I'll tell you why it's wrong. And this is what my gramma told me—Now you listen to me, Sandy. When Alfred was a kid, his dad stole some wood from old man Desjarlais. Now just listen for once. His dad never told him how he got the wood. So two weeks later Alfred was going by the Desjarlais, and they beat him so bad he couldn't walk. They took axe handles to that little kid. And you know something else? To this day, Alfred doesn't know the reasons why he got beat up. You can't hurt others, Sandy—to get back at someone else.

SANDY: Don't you understand? Can't you see what I've been through? I haven't done a thing about it all these years. You were right. And now when I'm finally gonna do something to hurt the man who hurt me, you're telling me to shut up and let him take my son? After what he did to me when I was a girl? And after what he's done to me all my goddamn life? I've had to work for that man—just so I could feed my kid a few scraps from his table. I've had to work for him, knowing what he's done to me. No. You got it wrong. He deserves to lose his boy after what he's put me through. And when I see that girl of Franky's, you can be sure I'm gonna tell her exactly what she's marrying into. That'll put an end to Alfred.

Light fades on MARTEN's shack.

Music up—fades.

Act Two

Scene One

> *Late Saturday afternoon. Music comes up with the lights on MARTEN's shack. The music will continue through the scene. MARTEN enters with his brand new axe. He's very pleased with his axe— swaggering as he tries carrying it in a variety of positions. He puts it over one shoulder then the other shoulder. He tries it out, carrying it in his right hand then the left. He goes through the motions—carefully and deliberately—of chopping wood, then of chopping down a tree. Finally, he checks out the sharpness of the blade–testing it against his finger. Out of the corner of his eye, he catches sight of his picnic table. Something clicks. He plunges the axe into the surface of the table. He gives the thumbs up. Lights and music down.*

Scene Two

> *Late Saturday afternoon. Music. Lights up on the kitchen. Music ends.*

FRANK: I thought that's what you wanted. I was doing this for you.

CLARA: For me? And I suppose you've already selected the colour of the house. For me. And I suppose you've decided that we're going to have a dog, and a cat, and 2.5 children. For me.

FRANK: Oh come on.

CLARA: I'm not being ridiculous. You've already gone ahead and bought the property. You've cleared the land where the house is going to be. You've practically got the house designed and built. And you've done all this behind my back without even asking whether I want to live there or not. Hello. You don't even have a wife yet.

FRANK: I had no idea you'd react like this. I thought you'd be happy.

CLARA: I know your intentions were good. But you can't go around making decisions for me. Is this what it's gonna be like?

FRANK: Like what? What do you mean?

CLARA: I thought I should tell you I've already bought a house in the city.

FRANK: You've what?

CLARA: And I've adopted two children, and you've got a dog named Rex.

FRANK: That's not the same thing.

CLARA: Then maybe you want to explain how it's not.

FRANK: For one thing, we talked about living outside the city.

CLARA: Outside the city, yes—but not in your dad's backyard.

FRANK: I got that land for twenty thousand—interest free.

CLARA: And that's another thing. You're spending money—

FRANK: I only had to put ten percent down.

CLARA: What about the payments?

FRANK: They don't start until next spring. And they're

almost nothing. You can't walk away from an offer like that. We could turn around tomorrow and sell it for three times the price.

CLARA: Good. Then sell it, and we'll get a house in town.

FRANK: Yes, we could sell that land for sixty thousand.

CLARA: It's halfway. I clocked it. You can drive here from there, and I can commute to the city.

FRANK: That's the homestead land. I spent my summers there till Grampa lost it and they started living here. Dad worked his ass off to get this land back. To hell if I'm gonna throw it out the window now.

CLARA: You're not listening—

FRANK: It's lakefront property. It's got soil for your garden. It can be whatever we want.

CLARA: No. Whatever you want. Or maybe what your father wants.

FRANK: What my father wants? You're saying that as if he's making all the decisions.

CLARA: Didn't he ask you about the land?

FRANK: No, I asked him about it. The only thing he said was that it'd be a "fine place to settle down and raise a family." And that was your idea.

CLARA: Yes, because having a family's important to me. You're forgetting I don't have a family.

FRANK: I'm not forgetting—

CLARA: My mother never had a choice. Robert got transferred to Regina. And he just said, "We're moving." And that's when they left me behind. Just like you did to me.

FRANK: When?

CLARA: When you went up north to article. You never told
             me until the week before you left—

FRANK: We've dealt with that—

CLARA: You left me in the dark for six months. I didn't
             know what to think—

FRANK: I was working. I was under a lot of pressure—

CLARA: Yes, but I never heard from you for four and a half
             months. What was I supposed to think?—

FRANK: Why are you bringing this up now?

CLARA: Because your decision—which you went ahead
             and made on your own—almost cost our
             relationship.

FRANK: This is different. I wanted this to bring us together.

CLARA: Frank. You can't just throw me into a situation
             where I don't have any control. Don't you
             understand? That's what I've been dealing with
             ever since my dad left.

             Slight pause.

FRANK: All right. I know what you mean. I'm sorry. I
             wasn't thinking—

CLARA: You weren't thinking about me.

FRANK: I was dealing with my dad, and if it had been
             anyone else, I wouldn't have gone ahead.

CLARA: You should have still asked me first.

FRANK: You're right. I should have asked you. And I
             shouldn't have done it without you.

CLARA: Do you mean that?

FRANK: Yes, I mean that.

CLARA: OK, then. C'mere. *(She reaches for his hand. They hug.)* That's better.

FRANK: Yeah.

CLARA: At least we've still got the rest of the weekend.

FRANK: Believe me, I didn't plan it like this.

CLARA: I know one thing for sure—it's gonna be just us tonight.

FRANK: That's what I was thinking. And tomorrow morning I'll bring you breakfast in bed. You can stay there all day if you like. I'll keep you company.

CLARA: I won't be staying there all day. We've got company coming.

FRANK: Who's coming?

CLARA: Sandy and Marie.

FRANK: What for?

CLARA: I invited them for coffee.

FRANK: When did you do that?

CLARA: When I was over at Marten's.

FRANK: Oh.

CLARA: Maybe after that we can go into town.

FRANK: Into town, for what?

CLARA: When I went through yesterday, I saw a few nice places. There was one in particular—that old stone house by the church?

FRANK: I know the one. But what are you suggesting?

CLARA: It's for sale.

FRANK: You're not still talking about living in town?

CLARA: Where else would we go? That's where your office is.

FRANK: But that's not where I want to live.

CLARA: I thought we just discussed that.

FRANK: Yes, and I just told you I should have talked to you first.

CLARA: That's right.

FRANK: But that doesn't mean that what I did was wrong—

CLARA: What do you mean it wasn't wrong? Of course it was wrong. You decided for me.

FRANK: That's the homestead land.

CLARA: I know that.

FRANK: If we're going to make it anywhere, it has to be here.

CLARA: What are you talking about?

FRANK: Buying that land was the right decision. How I went about it might of been wrong—

CLARA: That's fine. But I'm not living here on those terms.

FRANK: You knew how I felt about this community. You knew I was coming back here to practice law. And you knew I wanted you to be here. You've never questioned that. And now all of a sudden, you've turned on me.

CLARA: That's a lie, and you know it. You've put us into this position. And now you've got to make a decision.

FRANK: About what?

CLARA: About what you're going to do.

FRANK: And what is that?

CLARA: Frank, you have to give that land back to your dad.

FRANK: No, I don't—

CLARA: You have to—

FRANK: I can't do that—

CLARA: Frank!—

FRANK: Well then, fuck you.

            Pause.

CLARA: They told me this would happen.

FRANK: Who told you what?

CLARA: Sandy and Marie. They told me you'd change—
            once you "got" me here.

FRANK: Aw, come on—

CLARA: I can't believe that after two years of being
            together—

FRANK: And what else did they tell you? That I'm just like
            my dad? That I get drunk and chase women—

CLARA: Sandy said there was another woman.

FRANK: And who would that be?

CLARA: Marie. She said you spent a lot of time with her.

FRANK: That was years ago. She's married now. And yes
            we were close. We spent a lot of time together. But
            nothing ever happened.

CLARA: Frank—

FRANK: Nothing ever happened. We were just kids. Now
            you listen to me— I will never sell that land. And I
            plan on living there.

            Lights down as FRANK exits.

Scene Three

Saturday night. Lights up on MARTEN's shack. He's sitting at the table, picking at a nail sticking up from the table top. His axe is still in the table. He looks at the axe. Looks back at the nail. Picks up the axe near its head. Sizes up the situation then uses the blunt end of the axe to pound the nail—once, twice, and again for good measure. He feels the table top to see if the nail is flush. He sits down, apparently satisfied.

He sits for a moment then thinks of something. He reaches under the table to find out whether the nail has come through. He picks up the axe again and gives the nail a couple of whacks. Feels underneath again then sticks his head below to have a look.

While he's bending over, he notices that his bootlace is untied. He begins to tie his laces then stops. He unties his laces and takes off his boot. He tries to lift his leg up to smell his sock. He can't do it, so he takes off his sock. He holds the sock right up to his nose and smells it. He frowns.

He proceeds to take off his other boot and sock. Gets up and grabs a large glass salad bowl from inside another large tin bowl that contains his clean dishes. He sets the salad bowl on the table.

He goes to his five-gallon plastic pail and lifts it up, carrying it to the table. The pail is full of water to the brim. He tries to pour carefully, but he slops water all over. He sets the pail down and grabs his dish soap.

He squirts far too much soap into the bowl. Throws his socks in, the water darkening immediately. He works his socks in the bowl briefly. He takes them out and wrings them vigorously. He goes to his clothesline. He shakes the socks then holds them up.

He studies them for a moment, realizing that one sock is longer than the other. He turns and looks at the axe.

He walks to the table and lays his socks carefully on the table, side by side. Measures them up then picks up his axe. He's going to chop the end of the longer sock to make them the same length. He swings the axe but misses his target and cuts into both socks. He holds up the socks and both are dangling from where he chopped them. He lays them down on the table again to study the situation then hears a sound from outside.

He rushes to the window, peers out, then rushes to his battery light and unhooks it. Distant headlights shine through the window and fade. He waits for a moment. Hooks up the light again.

He returns to his socks. Picks up the axe, holding it carefully over his shoulder, aiming, aiming—then the chickens start squawking wildly.

MARTEN: The mink!

He rushes with his axe to the door. Stops. Looks down at his feet. He's barefoot. Starts to go back for his boots—but takes off outside anyway. Lights down. Chickens still squawking.

Scene Four

Saturday night. The fur shack. FRANK and ALFRED have been drinking rye, FRANK more than ALFRED. The bottle is near FRANK. ALFRED is cleaning a double-barreled shotgun. He's pulling a swab through the barrel. As the scene continues, he'll lightly oil the gun. The radio plays quietly.

ALFRED: I could see your Uncle Johnny there—as soon as he started calling, a big moose got up from under them bullrushes and—Bang!—over she went. He was yelling over to me and then damned if that cow didn't get up again. So Johnny pulled up and—Bang!—down she went. He thought for sure that was the end of it, but jesus christ if that cow didn't get back up and—Bang!—down she went a third time. When I finally got over to Johnny, he told me he had a helluva time getting that moose down—took three shots do it. So when we went over there, damned if there weren't three moose lying there side by side—

FRANK: I know, Dad—

ALFRED: I never told you that one—

FRANK: Yes, and you had to give one up. The game wardens said you were over the limit.

ALFRED: Well, I'm telling you, Franky, they don't understand us. We took that extra one in, and they wanted to charge us for poaching. We try to live an honest life and—

FRANK: Right, Dad.

He looks at FRANK then fixes a drink with ice.

ALFRED: Now what the hell's wrong with you? I been listening to you go on about that woman and about your house and that practice. They got Eugene put away, for chrissake, so stop worrying about your practice. And if that woman's got other plans, then let her go. She wouldn't stay for more than a couple of years anyway. You know, I'm starting to wonder about you. It's like that time you went out on the ice there to get that beaver—carrying on as if it was the end of the world. If you'd gone through that ice, I would of fished you out. It was only waist deep anyway. Hey?

FRANK has a shot and pours another.

You're a Métis. If you're gonna stay out here and take over from me, then you're gonna have to toughen up. You worry me when shit like that can get you so upset. I'm not gonna be around much longer. In five years time, I'm gonna have a lumber mill on old Murdock's land there. And we'll have a hundred head of cattle in the valley. And there'll be a big hotel and resort on the other side of Alfred Lake. I've got it all planned out, and if you're anything like me, you'll do just fine. Of course, you're only gonna be practicing law for another four or five years. Then you'll just have to concentrate on the business.

FRANK: And leave law?

ALFRED: You knew it would come to this. You can't make a decent living at it around here. No one's got any money.

FRANK sets his glass down sharply.

FRANK: You know something? I'm not like you. I can't hunt like you. I can't trap like you. And I sure as hell can't run a business like you. When I was out there on that ice, it was goddamn thin. I told you it was, and you still sent me back out there. I was seven years old, and if I'd gone through, there's no way you could of saved me. You would of fallen through before you got there, and I would of gone right under. And you know it. And you know something else? I did what you told me to. I got that beaver for you—and the few dollars it brought you for being willing to risk my life—

ALFRED: That's what I mean—you're soft. If we said anything like that when we were kids, we'd get the hell beat out of us. You've always been—

FRANK: Listen. Maybe I don't wanna take over. Maybe I just need a father because I never—

ALFRED: I gave you everything you needed. And maybe I shouldn't have.

FRANK: You didn't want nothing to do with me. That's why I came back. I came back for you—

ALFRED: I never spent my whole life here so you could come home and throw it all back in my face.

FRANK: That's not what I'm saying—

ALFRED: Don't you understand? You're next in line.

FRANK: You're talking as if you've got my whole life planned out. I never came back to take over—

ALFRED: I never thought I'd be stabbed in the back by my own son.

FRANK: What do you think these fucken papers are for?

             He points to the application papers.

ALFRED: Oh for chrissake, I don't care—

FRANK: For all I care, your business can go to hell!

             FRANK goes to leave.

ALFRED: You know something, Frank? I loved your mom.

             And all's I want to do is make things right.

             She told me she wanted you to have an education. And I swore to her the day she died I'd do that for you. Otherwise I would of kept you here.

             That's right. I was just keeping my promise to your mom.

             FRANK turns back.

             Now come on. You can't let me sit here by myself. Here.

ALFRED goes to pour a drink. FRANK stops him.

FRANK: I'll pour it myself.

ALFRED: That's better. Now I got something more to tell you. You gotta understand something, Franky.

You're getting it all. I'm leaving everything for you.

FRANK looks at his father as the lights fade.

Scene Five

Saturday night. Lights up on MARTEN's shack. His socks are hanging on the line. The trap is on the floor, and his mink lies on the table. MARTEN is aiming his axe like a gun at the deer calendar. He fires, making the appropriate sounds. He reloads as if he has a bolt-action gun. He fires again and reloads. EUGENE puts his head in the door and watches MARTEN fire again. EUGENE has a six pack of beer.

EUGENE: That's the easy part. Now you gotta gut it and skin it.

MARTEN is stunned for a moment and turns, pointing the axe at EUGENE.

Jesus christ, put the safety on that axe or you're gonna kill someone.

MARTEN: I got it, Eugene! I got it!

He darts to the table and displays the mink.

And it's a big one.

EUGENE: Yeah, he's got a few of your chickens in him.

MARTEN: Them chickens are having a party right now.

EUGENE: Well, you're lucky I'm not a game warden. Where's your trapper's licence?

MARTEN: I thought you were in jail.

EUGENE: You know they're never gonna catch me. Besides, I didn't do it.

MARTEN: I knew you didn't do it. I mean, you woulda taken the meat.

EUGENE sets the beer down and inspects the pelt.

EUGENE: Yeah, you'll get thirty-five bucks for this one.

MARTEN: I have to go tell Franky, so he can take me to Allbright's tomorrow.

EUGENE: Now now, Franky's not gonna be taking you anywhere.

MARTEN: What do you mean? He promised. He said he's gonna help me out now that he's back.

EUGENE: Franky told you that?

MARTEN: Yeah.

EUGENE: No no, he's not gonna have time for that. He's got his law practice and his dad to worry about. I'm gonna look after you. It was my idea to get you a gun, and I don't want Franky getting in trouble for it. There's been enough trouble already—starting with you.

MARTEN: What do you mean, me?

EUGENE: I had that talk with your mom the other day. I know there's been no one showing you how to hunt or what to do. And here you are, living in this shack, freezing your ass off every winter. That's why we're gonna fix it up for you. We're gonna get you some insulation, and I'm gonna pay to get a Hydro pole put in.

MARTEN: You mean I'm gonna have a flush toilet?

EUGENE: No, you're not gonna have a flush toilet. But you'll have a light switch and a plug-in. We'll get you a radio and Marie's old electric frying pan.

MARTEN: But I won't need them if I move in with Mom—

EUGENE: You're twenty-eight years old, for chrissake. You don't need to be moving in with your mom. Once you have a gun, you'll be able to feed yourself. You'll be a man. Now sit down here and you have one of these beers. I'm gonna tell you about having a gun. *(He opens two bottles and gives one to MARTEN.)* Now the reason I didn't go to jail was because I was honest when I went in there.

MARTEN: Yeah.

EUGENE: I told them straight up that I do take the odd deer. But it's for my family. Now Kid, you gotta remember—when you own a gun, you don't pick it up unless you're planning on killing something. And you use all the animal. That's how you respect them. And you always take a buck if you can, because it only takes one buck to breed all the does. And if you take a doe, you take all the children she could have. You got that?

MARTEN: Yeah.

EUGENE: Good. Now if you ever get caught poaching, you make sure you get over to my place and Marie will take that charge. You're gonna be a hunter, and we can't afford to lose a hunter. This is called sacrifice. This is what taking care of your community is. When you know there's someone looking after the community, you gotta protect them at all costs. Marie's been doing that for years and we've kept the family fed and half this community fed—like you and Sandy.

MARTEN: I can do that now.

EUGENE: That's right. Now if Franky did shoot that deer, and if Clara's a good woman—like I think she is—then she'll take that charge.

MARTEN: Clara's never even shot a gun. And she's scared of dead rabbits.

EUGENE: She'll have to take the charge. Now, I don't know if he shot that deer, but even if he did, we can't afford to have him getting charged. This is called loyalty. We've never had a lawyer sticking up for us, and we don't want our only lawyer going to jail. You understand that?

MARTEN: Well, what if he didn't shoot that deer?

EUGENE: Look, Kid. Those game wardens have got the bullet. And they told me it was a .30-30 that killed that buck. I don't own a .30-30, but Franky does. He's got it in the house. Now either he shot it or he lent it out. They didn't catch me, but them game wardens will be back tomorrow—

MARTEN starts putting on his boots.

Now where in the hell are you going?

MARTEN: I gotta go.

EUGENE: Now slow down there. You haven't even put your socks on.

MARTEN looks at his socks on the line.

MARTEN: They're wet.

EUGENE: You haven't told me where you're going.

MARTEN: I gotta see Franky.

EUGENE: About what?

MARTEN: I gotta warn him.

EUGENE:　　There's time for that in the morning.

MARTEN:　　I gotta tell him to hide his gun.

EUGENE:　　I was gonna call him, but if you wanna tell him, you can go first thing in the morning.

MARTEN:　　But I gotta tell him tonight.

EUGENE:　　He's not even there. He's with Alfred.

MARTEN stops what he's doing.

MARTEN:　　Alfred?

EUGENE:　　I seen his truck there on the way in. They're probably having a few drinks. Besides you got a beer to finish.

MARTEN:　　I'll go in the morning.

EUGENE:　　That's right.

MARTEN:　　And I'll take them over a chicken.

EUGENE:　　You do that.

EUGENE takes out the knife on his belt.

Now you sit down and skin this thing.

He opens the knife.

And get me a stretching board.

He holds up the mink.

Yeah, maybe you'll get forty bucks for it.

MARTEN:　　Forty bucks. I'll have enough for shells.

MARTEN gets a stretching board.

EUGENE:　　That's right. Tomorrow afternoon I'll take you over. And then you'll finally have your gun.

Lights down. Music.

Scene Six

Late Saturday night. The kitchen. FRANK comes in from his dad's. He stands, listening. Music fades. He starts for the bedroom but stops. He decides to go to the couch where he sits down, the weight of the world on him. He lets his head go back before eventually lying down. The couch is far too small. As he shifts, CLARA appears from the bedroom. She watches until he finally settles. She starts toward him, but he shifts, turning his back on her. She waits then returns to bed. He sits up.

Scene Seven

10 am, Sunday. Lights up on the kitchen. FRANK is asleep on the couch, still in his clothes. MARTEN enters and stops when he sees FRANK. He's carrying a small burlap bag with chicken feathers sticking to the outside. He looks at the bedroom and back at FRANK. He walks very quietly to the kitchen table and sets his bag on the table. He goes toward FRANK as if to wake him up. He stops, looks around, and then sees the .30-30 in the rack. He walks to the rack and gazes at the gun, admiring it. He runs a hand along the gun. He looks at FRANK, looks back at the gun, and then lifts it from the rack. He goes quickly to the door. The butt of the gun hits the door frame as he leaves. FRANK wakes up. He's not sure why. He sits up and holds his head. At last, he lifts his head, groggy, and stands. He sees the bag on the table. He opens the bag and grimaces. CLARA enters. She's dressed for the day. FRANK goes back toward the couch.

CLARA: Was it comfortable?

FRANK: Not really.

CLARA: Should we have some coffee?

FRANK: Go ahead.

CLARA: Do you want to talk?—

FRANK: What for?—

CLARA: Do you want to talk?—

FRANK: You're leaving anyway—

CLARA: Look, I don't want to argue.

FRANK: I don't want to argue either. I'm tired.

> *Pause.*

CLARA: Frank. What are we going to do?

FRANK: You've already made that decision, haven't you?

CLARA: Why are you talking to me like this?

FRANK: There's no point in this discussion.

CLARA: I need to know where we're at.

FRANK: Before doing what? You're already out the door.

CLARA: There's no use staying. I've hardly seen you this weekend. The first night here I spent with my back against the door, holding a gun. Last night I slept alone while you were out drinking. And that was after you revealed your grandiose plans for us yesterday—

FRANK: I told you already—I was just thinking about you.

CLARA: And I've told you already that if you'd been thinking about me—

FRANK: I know, I know, you don't have to tell me.

CLARA: All right then.

> *Brief pause.*

I'll be in the city. And when you're ready, please call me.

FRANK: You want me to call you?

CLARA: Yes. When you're ready.

FRANK: Ready for what? You're not gonna live here. My dad thinks I'm gonna take over where he left off—which I won't be doing—

CLARA: What are you talking about?

FRANK: I can't live someone else's life. Isn't that what you've been telling me? It's become quite apparent that I don't belong here. I'm gonna hand my cases over to McDiarmid in town. I'm gonna let Dad buy that land back. And I'm gonna go so far away...

Pause.

CLARA: Frank.

FRANK: Don't touch me. I don't need your sympathy. Yes, I'm guilty. I've made some big mistakes—but I won't be making them again.

CLARA: Is that it? You're giving up on everything?

FRANK: You don't understand. You were absolutely right yesterday. I'd only be hurting you more—

CLARA: It doesn't have to end here. I wasn't trying to destroy you. I wasn't trying to end our relationship. I was just trying to tell you what you needed to hear—for our sake.

FRANK: I'm sorry, Clara.

He moves toward the door.

CLARA: You can't leave.

FRANK: Isn't that what you were going to do?

CLARA: I was just leaving because the weekend hasn't
            worked out. That doesn't mean everything's
            finished.

FRANK: Yes, it does.

CLARA: So that's it then? You're just gonna walk out and
            throw it all away? Leave me behind. For my sake.
            Well, you know what? I've been through this
            before, and I know how it feels. It hurts. It hurts so
            much you can't even think. And all you want to do
            is crawl away— I know that feeling. And I'll tell
            you right now it doesn't work. It makes things
            worse. And I want you to remember, Frank—in
            case you've forgotten. You told me once—it was
            right after you'd come back from up north—you
            sat down and looked straight into my eyes—and
            you promised you'd never leave me. And I
            believed you. How can you do this to me? How can
            you hurt me like this?

FRANK: Clara…

CLARA: No. I don't want to hear you. Just get in that truck
            and go. I'll be gone when you get back.

            Go on.

            Get out.

            *CLARA turns away. FRANK exits. CLARA
            collapses on a chair at the table. She closes her eyes,
            and when she opens them again, she is staring
            straight at the bag on the table. She picks it up as if
            to look inside and finds a pool of blood underneath it.
            She drops the bag in disgust and rushes into the
            bedroom. She returns with her bags. She stops by
            the door and sees the gun missing from the rack just
            as SANDY and MARIE enter.*

SANDY: So you're taking my advice.

MARIE: You're not leaving already, are you?

CLARA: I have to get back.

SANDY: Without saying goodbye? What about the coffee?

CLARA: I'm sorry, I don't have time—

SANDY: Neither does Franky. He sure took off in a hurry. I'd say he was off to a fire—or maybe you two had a fight.

MARIE: Let's put those suitcases away—

CLARA: I can't—

MARIE: And sit down.

SANDY: No no, let her go. She's done. Franky will bring another one home.

CLARA: You don't know what you're talking about.

MARIE: Come on, Clara—

CLARA: I've got work to do. I can't stay.

SANDY: Good. Close the door on your way out.

CLARA sets down her bags.

MARIE: Do you have to be so ignorant?

SANDY: I'm complimenting her. It's only taken her a weekend to see what this place is like. She's smarter than I thought she was.

MARIE: So what's that saying about you? You've never left. Now just shut up, Sandy, and sit down.

CLARA: There's no use talking about it.

MARIE: What happens around here is all our business. So how come you're leaving early?

CLARA: It's just what I said.

MARIE: That's not it. Now what happened?

CLARA: I never saw him all weekend, that's what happened.

MARIE: There's more to it than that.

CLARA: What do you want to know? He showed me the land he bought from his dad.

MARIE: Yeah?

CLARA: And he wanted us to live there.

MARIE: What did you want?

CLARA: That's just it—he never asked me what I wanted. I thought we were buying a house in town.

MARIE: So that's why he left?

CLARA: I told him to sell the land back to his dad.

SANDY: That's the homestead land. You'll be lucky if he comes back at all.

CLARA: He's not coming back. He's giving it up, and he's quitting his practice. It's over.

MARIE: So it's all because you didn't want to live on that piece of land?

CLARA: No, his dad wanted him to take over, and he didn't want to.

SANDY: I knew that's what that bastard was up to. If he'd known his dad better, he'd have never come back. It's just as well he's leaving.

CLARA: How can you say that? He was committed to this community.

SANDY: So you're taking his side now? It seems to me you're the one that's not committed. You don't want to live here.

CLARA: I never said I didn't want to live here. It was the way he forced it on me.

SANDY: Ohh, so he's to blame.

CLARA: He didn't want to talk about it. Now he's throwing it all away.

SANDY: Including you.

MARIE: He's running away from himself.

CLARA: That's it exactly. And he's done this to me once before.

SANDY: Oh, you poor girl.

CLARA: Why are you so obnoxious? What have I done to you?

SANDY: I've seen your kind before. You're crying as if you got something to cry about. Well, you know what? You don't know nothing.

CLARA: You don't know anything about me. You must think I've led some kind of sheltered life. Well, I haven't. I've been on my own since I was twelve.

SANDY: Is that right?

CLARA: That's right.

SANDY: So let's hear it—

CLARA: Oh god—

SANDY: Come on.

CLARA: My dad deserted us, if you want to know the truth.

SANDY: Uh huh—

CLARA: And my mother fell apart. I had to look after her cause she wouldn't leave the house. She couldn't get out of bed. I've gone through hell because my dad ran away. And now I have to go through it again? With Frank?

She goes for her bags.

MARIE: Come on, Clara.

CLARA: Just get out of my way.

MARIE: No no, you're gonna make it worse.

CLARA: How can it get any worse?

MARIE: You'll sit in that house just like your mom did. And you'll drive yourself crazy thinking about it. "If only it could have been different."

CLARA: Nothing's going to change.

MARIE: Yes, it will because there's too much at stake. You and Frank need each other, and you know it. He's got work to do here. And so do you.

CLARA: Me.

MARIE: Yes, you. And besides, you don't know the whole story yet.

CLARA: What story.

MARIE: Sandy came over here this morning to tell you something. Isn't that right, Sandy.

SANDY: What?

MARIE: Go ahead.

SANDY: What, she's leaving.

MARIE: Not until she hears what you have to say.

SANDY: What difference is it gonna make? I don't need to tell her now. She's going back to the city and Franky's leaving.

MARIE: You made your decision yesterday. You were gonna tell her for different reasons. But things have changed.

SANDY: How?

MARIE: She's just like you, Sandy. She's been on her own for a long time. Now you tell her. If she goes back to the city after that, that's fine. But she has to hear it first.

Pause.

SANDY: I don't know what to say.

MARIE: Now that's the first time I ever heard you saying that.

SANDY: I can't do this.

MARIE: Yes, you can.

SANDY: I don't know where I'd start.

Pause. CLARA moves impatiently.

MARIE: Are you going to tell her before she goes?

SANDY: I guess so.

MARIE: Then tell her about when you first got here. You were ten years old.

SANDY: That's right.

MARIE: Coming in to a Métis community.

Pause.

Where were your mom and dad?

SANDY: My dad was in jail.

MARIE: What for?

SANDY: He stole a tractor.

MARIE: What about your mom?

SANDY: She was living with the bootlegger. Eddie Constant. He already had eight kids—so he didn't want nothing to do with me.

MARIE: So what did you do?

SANDY: I had to quit school. I was about twelve— and then I started driving truck. Mostly I was hauling hay for Franky's dad. Even though he never paid me. He never paid anyone. He'd pay Marie's dad with a box of groceries and then he'd throw in a case of beer. That's how he got rich. He was only twenty-five, and he'd already made his money. If you didn't work for him, you just didn't work. And that's the way it still is. I'm still working for Alfred—up there painting his house and weeding his garden.

           Pause.

           That's it.

MARIE: What else?

SANDY: Nothing.

MARIE: Hey?

           Pause.

SANDY: I didn't have nowhere else to go. I was ten. And I was on my own. I guess you know what that's like.

           He took me to Saskatoon one time. I was thirteen that year. He put me in his truck and off we went.

           We stayed at the Senator. And he got me room service. I had a cheeseburger and a chocolate milkshake. Then he brought out the Five Star–and then he got me drunk. And then he climbed up on top of me.

Pause.

The next day he told me to get myself cleaned up. And then he put me in the truck, and we came right back here.

Pause.

But that's not the half of it. He got me pregnant. Mom and Eddie told him I was his now. "You look after that girl or she'll be going to a home." Then about three or four months later, he told me, "Come on, you get in the truck. We're going back to Saskatoon." So I got up and got ready and never asked any questions. He took me to this doctor. He had an office in his house. "You go in there now, and this doctor's gonna give you something." That doctor must of pumped about six needles into me. And then I took pills on top of that for seven days. That was supposed to fix it. But it didn't. Because about five months later, I had my baby.

Pause.

That's when I had Marten.

Pause.

That's what I came to tell you. I came to tell you about Franky's dad.

CLARA:	Alfred.
SANDY:	That's right. That's Marten's dad.
CLARA:	So…
SANDY:	Marten and Franky are half-brothers.
CLARA:	So how come Frank's never told me that?
MARIE:	He doesn't know.
CLARA:	He doesn't know? Then why are you telling me?

MARIE: If you're gonna be with Franky, you have to know what happened.

CLARA: Yes, but why tell me before you tell him? I mean, it's his father.

MARIE: You're right. Alfred should have been the one. But he never. He kept it from him. How was Alfred gonna tell him something like that?

CLARA: So you weren't going to tell him either?

MARIE: I never said that.

SANDY: You gotta understand something. Alfred's always threatened to take away my son. I couldn't let that happen.

CLARA: So who else knows.

SANDY: Everyone knows. But they don't talk about it.

CLARA: You mean, everyone knows but Frank.

SANDY: And Marten. I've never told him neither.

CLARA: Yet you can tell me. It's like you're putting Frank's life in my hands. How can I tell him something like that? I can't stay with him now.

MARIE: Don't you see? That's the only way that you can.

CLARA: I can't believe you'd do this to me. After all that's happened this weekend.

MARIE: He can't go running off now.

CLARA: How's this supposed to keep him here?

MARIE: He can't be allowed to take over from his dad. Yet he still has to be here.

CLARA: Really.

MARIE: And you're the one he has to rely on.

CLARA: Me.

MARIE: You don't understand it yet. But you will. Franky's told me all about you.

CLARA: What did he tell you?

MARIE: He told me what kind of person you are. He said you understand him. Clara. Look at him. He can't make it here on his own. He needs someone other than his dad.

> *Pause. MARTEN enters, followed by ALFRED. ALFRED is carrying the .30-30.*

ALFRED: Look what I found walking around with my .30-30. I was almost too scared to go get him. Does he belong to anyone here?

SANDY: What the hell you up to now? And how'd you get that gun?

ALFRED: He was crossing the field by the Lake Road, right near where he almost shot me that time. I chased him down with my truck and brung him in.

SANDY: Did you take that gun?

ALFRED: He got it from here.

SANDY: He got the gun from here? Is that true? *(To CLARA.)*

CLARA: Maybe Frank gave it to him.

ALFRED: No, I don't think Franky woulda gave him the gun—at least not this one.

SANDY: I don't know what the hell's going on here—

ALFRED: That's obvious. Your kid is out of control. He should stick to those chickens I bought him. I got him a new axe, and that's not enough.

SANDY: Did Franky give you that gun?

ALFRED: He clammed right up and refused to tell me anything. If I hadn't stopped him, he'd have been in town by supper.

SANDY: He was going to town?

ALFRED: He might have been on his way to Jake Munson's— to get some shells.

SANDY: What's gotten into you?

ALFRED: You're not gonna get anything outta him. But maybe the police can.

SANDY: You let me deal with this.

MARIE: Maybe it's not the police we should be calling. I think Marten knows exactly what he's doing.

                 FRANK enters.

SANDY: Did you give my kid that gun? So help me god, if you gave him that gun—

ALFRED: For chrissake, just shut up. Of course, he took it. I found him on the Lake Road with it. *(To FRANK.)*

SANDY: He'll tell me what's happened when he's good and ready. I'll get to the bottom of it when I get him home.

ALFRED: No one's leaving here until we get the truth. And if we don't, I'll be picking up that phone, and he'll be spending the night in jail.

SANDY: He will not be spending the night in jail. And if you call the police, I'll take that gun and shoot you myself.

FRANK: What the hell is going on here?

ALFRED: The Kid took your grampa's .30-30, that's what.

FRANK: Is that right? Marten, did you take my gun?

SANDY: I said I was gonna—

FRANK: Marten. Look at me. Did you take my gun?

                MARTEN looks at MARIE.

MARIE: You tell him.

                Pause.

MARTEN: I brought Clara her chicken this morning.

CLARA: That's right. He left it right there.

MARTEN: And Franky, you were sleeping.

SANDY: You don't need to tell them anything.

MARIE: Let him go, Sandy.

MARTEN: I had to do it.

FRANK: You can't go around stealing guns. We were gonna get you one.

ALFRED: What do you mean, you had to?

MARTEN: I shot the deer.

SANDY: You shot the deer? Just for the horns? Oh my god!

FRANK: That was a stupid fucken thing to do. You'll never own a gun now. What were you thinking?

ALFRED: I told you he was out of control. Take him home.

FRANK: You stole that gun twice? That means he took it from you first. *(To ALFRED.)*

ALFRED: I guess he must of.

SANDY: We're closing up that shack, and you're moving back in with me. Ever since you moved out, it's been one thing after another.

FRANK: So you were gonna go shoot another one today. Is that it?

MARTEN: I wasn't gonna shoot nothing. I was going to the game wardens.

SANDY: Jesus christ. (*SANDY turns away.*)

FRANK: For what?

MARTEN: I have to tell em I shot it.

FRANK: Which would get Eugene out.

MARTEN: No. Eugene's out.

FRANK: When did he get out?

MARIE: He was never in. They just took him in for questioning.

MARTEN: They were gonna blame you.

FRANK: Blame me? For what?

MARTEN: I used that gun. And you had it.

ALFRED: Sounds like the case is closed. You're the lawyer here. You better take him in.

FRANK: I can't help him.

CLARA: Frank, you could take him—

FRANK: No, I'm not taking him anywhere.

CLARA: But—

FRANK: And you can just stay out of this.

SANDY: I'll take him in.

MARIE: No. He's not going anywhere. Marten. It's time you told the truth.

MARTEN: That's the truth.

MARIE: Where'd you get the shells?

MARTEN blinks, confused.

Where'd you put the horns?

He tries to say something.

How come you never took the meat? You know very well you have to take the meat.

MARTEN: I had to take that charge for Franky.

FRANK: I never shot that deer.

MARTEN: Cause he would of lost his job and—

FRANK: I'm telling you, Kid. I never shot that deer.

MARTEN: But you had the .30-30.

SANDY: How do you know that was the gun?

FRANK: I never had it till after that deer was shot.

ALFRED: It coulda been any .30-30 in the country.

MARIE: I don't think so. Actually, he was trying to protect you. *(To ALFRED.)* Isn't that right, Marten?

                    Pause.

MARTEN: I had to protect him.

FRANK: Who?

MARTEN: Alfred.

FRANK: He shot that deer?

MARTEN: I had to protect my dad.

FRANK: Who?

MARTEN: My dad.

FRANK: Marten. Your dad's dead.

MARTEN: No he's not.

                    He looks at ALFRED.

FRANK: What are you looking at him for?

ALFRED: You people are all fucked. You can't leave well enough alone. And you? *(To MARIE.)* You're sick.

SANDY: You told him. *(To MARIE.)*

MARIE: I never told him nothing.

SANDY: Somebody must of told him.

FRANK: Told him what?

MARIE: Let him tell you. Go ahead, Marten.

MARTEN: Jim Shingoose told me.

FRANK: What'd he tell you?

MARTEN: He told me my dad got a good deal on that shack. Alfred got me that shack.

ALFRED: Oh, what does it matter.

FRANK: Well, it matters a lot. This has all gotta be sorted out. You goddamn whore—I never believed those stories about you.

SANDY: You believe everything he tells you, don't you?

FRANK: I know what your reputation is.

SANDY: If you knew what he did to me, you'd take that back. That man's been lying to you for years, and you've had your head shoved up your—

FRANK: You shut up—

SANDY: Franky. Listen to me. I was thirteen years old.

FRANK: What are you talking about?

SANDY: I was thirteen years old when it happened. You figure it out. He's your father.

                Pause.

FRANK: Is that right?

ALFRED turns away.

You did that to her when she was thirteen? Is that why you sent me away? Hey? Well, you know what. I heard that one too. I heard it years ago—from little Billy Desjarlais. And I went after him for saying that retarded kid was my brother. That was disgusting. How could he insult my dad like that? Putting him in bed with that Sandy Scott. And now I find out it's true, and she was thirteen years old?—

ALFRED: Now come on, Franky. You don't know what you're saying.

EUGENE enters.

EUGENE: So what do we got going on here?

ALFRED: I'm on my way out.

EUGENE: So soon? What have you done for us this time?

ALFRED goes to leave, taking the gun.

ALFRED: You people don't know what you're doing here. After everything I've done for you. Don't you understand? No?

ALFRED turns to go.

FRANK: You're taking that?

ALFRED: I'm taking my gun.

FRANK: You just gave it away.

ALFRED: Take your gun back then.

He hands it to FRANK.

FRANK: No. You keep it—I don't want it. How can I take it from you now?

EUGENE: You better take it, Alfred. The game wardens are down there looking for you, and they want to see that gun—and your collection of horns. I know you got the best collection around here– but you won't be adding to it this time.

             ALFRED exits with the gun.

             Now what's everyone looking so glum for? Hey?

             FRANK goes to the door. CLARA moves to him.

             Now, you hold on there. I don't know if you all know this. But the Kid here.

             EUGENE puts his arm around MARTEN.

             He got his mink last night!—

SANDY: Jesus christ—

EUGENE: And he's gonna get his gun!—

SANDY: Like hell he is! That kid's got his chickens to look after!

             Lights down.

Scene Eight

             Lights up on the fur shack. ALFRED's gun is on the table beside the antlers. He's at the table, his application papers open. He finishes reading a passage. He pours a drink. He sets the glass down then sweeps the papers off the table. He holds up the antlers and tries to snap them. His face, behind the antlers, shows the rage he's had for his entire life. The lights fade, isolating him, until all we see is his face and the antlers.

Scene Nine

> *Lights up on the kitchen, FRANK and CLARA together on the couch.*

EUGENE: No, Sandy. He's not moving back in with you. It's not right.

SANDY: He was just living there until I got the Murdock place.

EUGENE: That's years away.

SANDY: No, it won't be. I'll be in there this spring and you better be there with your truck to help me.

EUGENE: I told him we're gonna fix up that shack. You watch. That kid'll be living in the lap of luxury by the time we get done. Isn't that right, Franky?

FRANK: What.

EUGENE: All it's gonna take is a couple of days and a little bit of money. Franky will be there.

SANDY: Well, if that's the case, I don't wanna see any half-ass job. It's gonna need curtains and some paint on them walls. And Clara can help out too.

CLARA: Pardon me?

MARIE: Only if you want to, Clara.

EUGENE: See? Your mom says it's OK. We'll do an estimate as soon as we're back from Allbright's.

SANDY: Allbright's? That's going too far. There'll be no gun in that house.

MARTEN: But Mom—

EUGENE: You gotta let him go sometime. He's ready.

SANDY: No, he's not ready.

MARTEN: I'm not a kid any more. I'm almost thirty.

MARIE: He's right, Sandy. If he's not ready now, he never
             will be. We're here if he needs us.

             FRANK and CLARA go to leave.

EUGENE: Hey hey, where you guys going now?

FRANK: Well—we were going out for a walk.

EUGENE: When are you coming back?

FRANK: I don't know.

EUGENE: You better be back before supper.

CLARA: We'll be back before then.

EUGENE: Are you sure?

FRANK: Don't worry about us. We'll be fine.

MARIE: That's good. Cause someone's gotta eat that
             chicken.

             FRANK and CLARA exit.

EUGENE: Yeah, there's no meat left at our house neither—
             cause the kids burnt all the baloney too.

MARTEN: We don't need no baloney. Them grain-fed
             chickens I got are real good. And Mom knows how
             to make the best stuffing.

SANDY: Now about that gun.

             Lights begin to fade.

EUGENE: Yeah, what about it?

SANDY: If I let you take that boy up to Allbright's.

EUGENE: Yeah?

SANDY: You gotta promise you'll keep those shells at your place.

EUGENE: I got no problem with that.

MARTEN: That's OK with me.

SANDY: And when he gets his first deer, you make sure I get the liver. And there'll be no meat hanging in that shack. It's his house now.

                MARTEN goes to leave.

                Now where you running off to?

MARTEN: I gotta go kill some more chickens.

SANDY: What for?

MARTEN: Them kids at Eugene and Marie's gotta have something to eat too. They got no baloney even.

SANDY: OK, off you go. I'll be down to get em plucked.

MARTEN: And plus I gotta skin that mink. I'll skin him out and then I'll stretch him real good and tight.

EUGENE: You do that, Kid. You do that.

                Lights down.

                Music.

                The End.